EDEXCEL INTERNATIONAL GCSE (9–1)

HISTORY

CHINA: CONFLICT, CRISIS AND CHANGE, 1900–89

Student Book

Sarah Moffatt

Series Editor: Nigel Kelly

Published by Pearson Education Limited, 80 Strand, London, WC2R 0RL.

www.pearsonglobalschools.com

Copies of official specifications for all Pearson qualifications may be found on the website: https://qualifications.pearson.com

Text © Pearson Education Limited 2017
Edited by Juliet Gardner
Designed by Cobalt id and Pearson Education Limited
Typeset and illustrated by Phoenix Photosetting, Chatham, Kent
Original illustrations © Pearson Education Limited 2017
Cover design by Pearson Education Limited
Picture research by Andreas Schindler
Cover photo/illustration Mary Evans Picture Library: Everett Collection
Inside front cover Shutterstock.com: Dmitry Lobanov

The rights of Sarah Moffatt to be identified as author of this work have been asserted by her in accordance with the Copyright, Designs and Patents Act 1988.

First published 2017

19 18
10 9 8 7 6 5 4 3

British Library Cataloguing in Publication Data
A catalogue record for this book is available from the British Library

ISBN 978 0 435 18537 4

Printed in Slovakia by Neografia

Picture Credits
The publisher would like to thank the following for their kind permission to reproduce their photographs:
(Key: b-bottom; c-centre; l-left; r-right; t-top)

Alamy Stock Photo: age fotostock 12bl, Dennis Cox 94tr, CPRESS PHOTO LIMITED 80c, Everett Collection Historical 35cr, 43cr, 49br, 70tr, Eye Ubiquitous 92cr, Granger Historical Picture Archive 37tr, Granger, NYC. 26tr, Peter Horree 72tc, ITAR-TASS Photo Agency 61tr, 97tr, Keystone Pictures USA 88cl, Mary Evans Picture Library 59tr, Photo 12 44cr, LEE SNIDER 75bl, World History Archive 13bl **Bridgeman Art Library Ltd:** Poster, 'The revolution is not yet completed; your comrades must continue to make efforts', 1927 (colour litho), Chinese School, (20th century) / British Library, London, UK / © British Library Board. All Rights Reserved / Bridgeman Images 16b **Getty Images:** Fox Photos 23, Hulton Archive 2, Keystone 85, PhotoQuest 41, Sovfoto / UIG 65 **Rex Shutterstock:** Martyn Goddard 92tl, SIPA PRESS 255550 67br, The Art Archive 53t, 57tr, Universal History Archive 6tc, Universal History Archive / Universal Images Group 8cl **TopFoto:** 25bl, AP 96c, Granger, NYC 9c, 14br, 32tr, Topham / AP 86cr, Topham Picturepoint 68br, ullstein-bild 18cr, 30tl, 47c

All other images © Pearson Education

Figures
We are grateful to the following for permission to reproduce copyright material:
Figures on pages 4, 29 adapted from Empire to People's Republic 1900–49, 2nd ed, Michael Lynch, Hodder Education. Reproduced by permission of Hodder Education.; Figure on page 46 adapted from Access to History: The People's Republic of China 1949-76, 2nd ed. Michael Lynch. Reproduced by permission of Hodder Education

Text
Extract on page 10 from China: From Empire to People's Republic 1900–49, 2nd ed, Michael Lynch, Hodder Education. Reproduced by permission of Hodder Education; Extract on page 13, J. Fenby, 2012, The Penguin History of Modern China, Penguin, no amendment should be made to the text without the written permission of David Higham Associates Limited.; Extract on page 27 from The Morning Deluge: Mao Tsetung and the Chinese Revolution, 1893- 1954 by Han Suyin Copyright 1972. Re-printed by kind permission of the Han Suyin Trust for Scientific Exchange.; Extract on page 30 from China Since 1900, Josh Brooman, 1988, Pearson Education Limited; Extracts on pages 31, 42 from AQA A LEV HIST TRANSFORMATION OF CHINA by Robert Whitfield (OUP, 2015). Extract used by permission of Oxford University Press, UK.; Extract on page 45 from Wild Swans, Jung Chang, 1991. Reprinted by permis-sion of HarperCollins Publishers Ltd and Copyright: Jung Chang, 1991; Extract on page 50 from China Since 1900, Josh Brooman, 1988, Pearson Education Limited; Extracts on pages 57, 67 from THE PRIVATE LIFE OF CHAIRMAN MAO by Dr. Zhi-Sui Li, copyright © 1995 by Dr. Zhi-Sui Li. Published by Chatto & Windus used by permission of Random House, an imprint and division of and Penguin Random House LLC. All rights reserved.; Extract on page 71 republished with permission of Taylor & Francis Group LLC Books, from Shades of Mao: The Posthumous Cult of the Great Leader, Barmé, G.R., 1996, 'A Star Reflects on the Sun' by Liu Xiaoqing, 1996; permission conveyed through Copyright Clearance Centre, Inc.; Extract on page 73 from Frank Dikotter, 2016, The Cultural Revolution: A People's History 1962-76, Bloomsbury Publishing Plc.; Extract on page 74 from RED AZALEA by Anchee Min, copyright © 1994 by Anchee Min. Bloomsbury Publishing Plc. Used by permission of Pantheon Books, an imprint of the Knopf Doubleday Publishing Group, a division and of Penguin Random House LLC. All rights reserved.; Extract on page 75 from Peking Review, No. 2, 10 January 1969; Extract on page 92 Copyright Guardian News & Me-dia Ltd 2017; Extract on page 93 from Mao's China 1936-97, Michael Lynch, 2015, Hodder Education. Reproduced by permission of Hodder Education; Extracts on pages 95, 98 from THE SEARCH FOR MODERN CHINA, A DOCUMENTARY COL-LECTION by Pei Kai Cheng, Michael Lestz and Jonathan Spence. Copyright © 1999 by W. W. Norton & Company, Inc. Used by permission of W. W. Norton & Company, Inc.; Extract on page 98 from J. Fenby, 2012, The Penguin History of Modern China, Penguin, no amendment should be made to the text without the written permission of David Higham Associates Limited.

Select glossary terms have been taken from *The Longman Dictionary of Contemporary English Online*.

Disclaimer
All maps in this book are drawn to support the key learning points. They are illustrative in style and are not exact representations.

Endorsement Statement
In order to ensure that this resource offers high-quality support for the associated Pearson qualification, it has been through a review process by the awarding body. This process confirms that this resource fully covers the teaching and learning content of the specification or part of a specification at which it is aimed. It also confirms that it demonstrates an appropriate balance between the development of subject skills, knowledge and understanding, in addition to preparation for assessment.

Endorsement does not cover any guidance on assessment activities or processes (e.g. practice questions or advice on how to answer assessment questions) included in the resource nor does it prescribe any particular approach to the teaching or delivery of a related course.

While the publishers have made every attempt to ensure that advice on the qualification and its assessment is accurate, the official specification and associated assessment guidance materials are the only authoritative source of information and should always be referred to for definitive guidance.

Pearson examiners have not contributed to any sections in this resource relevant to examination papers for which they have responsibility.

Examiners will not use endorsed resources as a source of material for any assessment set by Pearson. Endorsement of a resource does not mean that the resource is required to achieve this Pearson qualification, nor does it mean that it is the only suitable material available to support the qualification, and any resource lists produced by the awarding body shall include this and other appropriate resources.

ABOUT THIS BOOK

This book is written for students following the Pearson Edexcel International GCSE (9–1) History specification and covers one unit of the course. This unit is China: Conflict, Crisis and Change, 1900–89, one of the Breadth Studies.

The History course has been structured so that teaching and learning can take place in any order, both in the classroom and in any independent learning. The book contains five chapters which match the five areas of content in the specification:

- The fall of the Qing, warlordism and chaos, 1900–34
- The triumph of Mao and the CCP, 1934–49
- Change under Mao, 1949–63
- The Cultural Revolution and its impact, 1965–76
- China, 1976–89

Each chapter is split into multiple sections to break down content into manageable chunks and to ensure full coverage of the specification.

Each chapter features a mix of learning and activities. Sources are embedded throughout to develop your understanding and exam-style questions help you to put learning into practice. Recap pages at the end of each chapter summarise key information and let you check your understanding. Exam guidance pages help you prepare confidently for the exam.

Learning Objectives Each section starts with a list of what you will learn in it. They are carefully tailored to address key assessment objectives central to the course.

Source
Photos, cartoons and text sources are used to explain events and show you what people from the period said, thought or created, helping you to build your understanding.

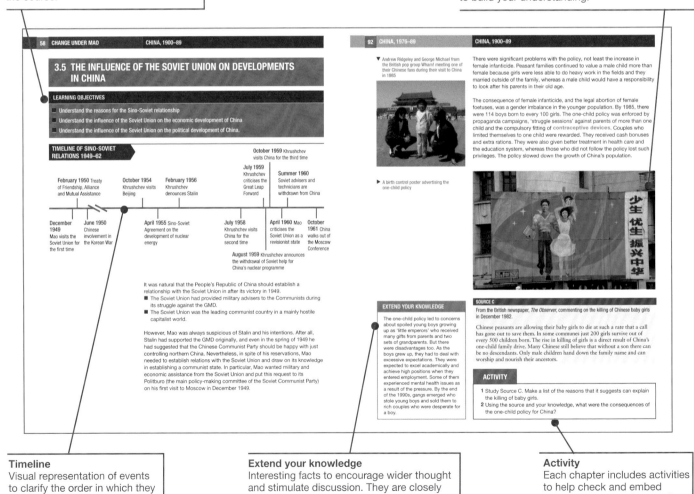

Timeline
Visual representation of events to clarify the order in which they happened.

Extend your knowledge
Interesting facts to encourage wider thought and stimulate discussion. They are closely related to key issues and allow you to add depth to your knowledge and answers.

Activity
Each chapter includes activities to help check and embed knowledge and understanding.

Recap
At the end of each chapter, you will find a page designed to help you consolidate and reflect on the chapter as a whole.

Recall quiz
This quick quiz is ideal for checking your knowledge or for revision.

Key term
Useful words and phrases are colour coded within the main text and picked out in the margin with concise and simple definitions. These help understanding of key subject terms and support students whose first language is not English.

Exam-style question
Questions tailored to the Pearson Edexcel specification to allow for practice and development of exam writing technique. They also allow for practice responding to the command words used in the exams.

Skills
Relevant exam questions have been assigned the key skills which you will gain from undertaking them, allowing for a strong focus on particular academic qualities. These transferable skills are highly valued in further study and the workplace.

Hint
All exam-style questions are accompanied by a hint to help you get started on an answer.

Checkpoint
Checkpoints help you to check and reflect on your learning. The Strengthen section helps you to consolidate knowledge and understanding, and check that you have grasped the basic ideas and skills. The Challenge questions push you to go beyond just understanding the information, and into evaluation and analysis of what you have studied.

Summary
The main points of each chapter are summarised in a series of bullet points. These are great for embedding core knowledge and handy for revision.

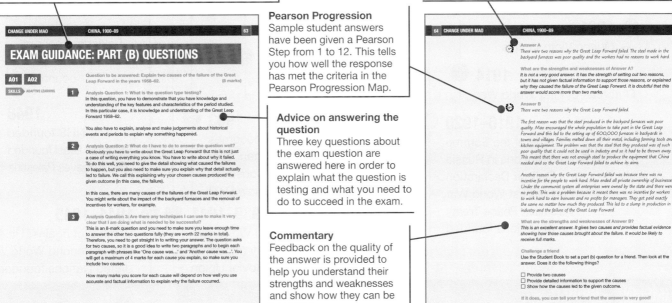

Exam guidance
At the end of each chapter, you will find two pages designed to help you better understand the exam questions and how to answer them. Each exam guidance section focuses on a particular question type that you will find in the exam, allowing you to approach them with confidence.

Pearson Progression
Sample student answers have been given a Pearson Step from 1 to 12. This tells you how well the response has met the criteria in the Pearson Progression Map.

Advice on answering the question
Three key questions about the exam question are answered here in order to explain what the question is testing and what you need to do to succeed in the exam.

Commentary
Feedback on the quality of the answer is provided to help you understand their strengths and weaknesses and show how they can be improved.

Student answers
Exemplar student answers are used to show what an answer to the exam question may look like. There are often two levels of answers so you can see what you need to do to write better responses.

TIMELINE – CHINA: CONFLICT, CRISIS AND CHANGE, 1900–89

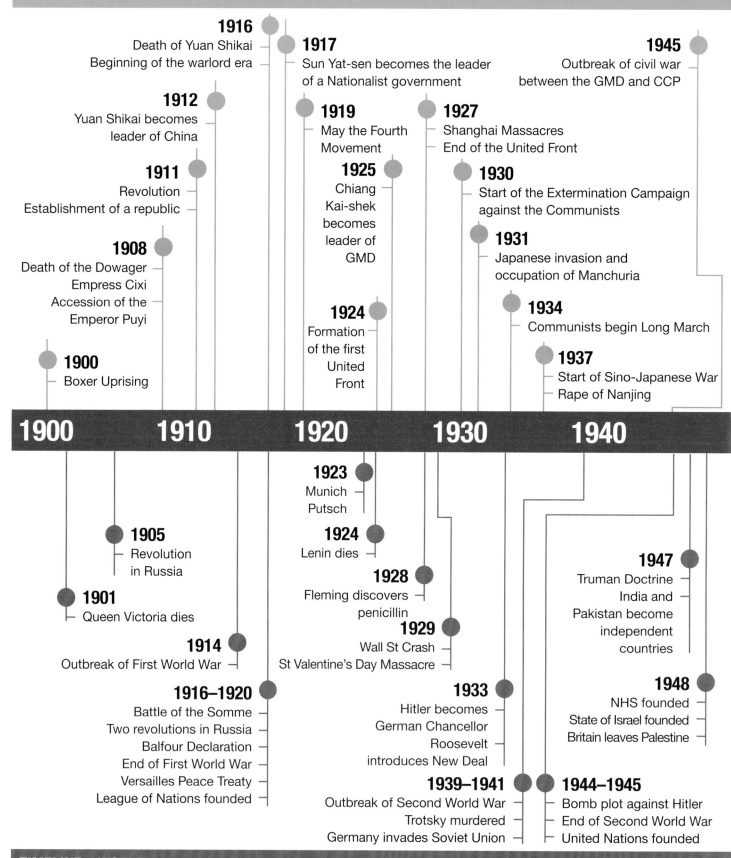

1916
Death of Yuan Shikai
Beginning of the warlord era

1917
Sun Yat-sen becomes the leader
of a Nationalist government

1945
Outbreak of civil war
between the GMD and CCP

1912
Yuan Shikai becomes
leader of China

1919
May the Fourth
Movement

1927
Shanghai Massacres
End of the United Front

1911
Revolution
Establishment of a republic

1925
Chiang
Kai-shek
becomes
leader of
GMD

1930
Start of the Extermination Campaign
against the Communists

1908
Death of the Dowager
Empress Cixi
Accession of the
Emperor Puyi

1931
Japanese invasion and
occupation of Manchuria

1924
Formation
of the first
United
Front

1934
Communists begin Long March

1900
Boxer Uprising

1937
Start of Sino-Japanese War
Rape of Nanjing

1900   **1910**   **1920**   **1930**   **1940**

1923
Munich
Putsch

1905
Revolution
in Russia

1924
Lenin dies

1901
Queen Victoria dies

1947
Truman Doctrine
India and
Pakistan become
independent
countries

1928
Fleming discovers
penicillin

1914
Outbreak of First World War

1929
Wall St Crash
St Valentine's Day Massacre

1916–1920
Battle of the Somme
Two revolutions in Russia
Balfour Declaration
End of First World War
Versailles Peace Treaty
League of Nations founded

1933
Hitler becomes
German Chancellor
Roosevelt
introduces New Deal

1948
NHS founded
State of Israel founded
Britain leaves Palestine

1939–1941
Outbreak of Second World War
Trotsky murdered
Germany invades Soviet Union

1944–1945
Bomb plot against Hitler
End of Second World War
United Nations founded

TIMELINE – WORLD

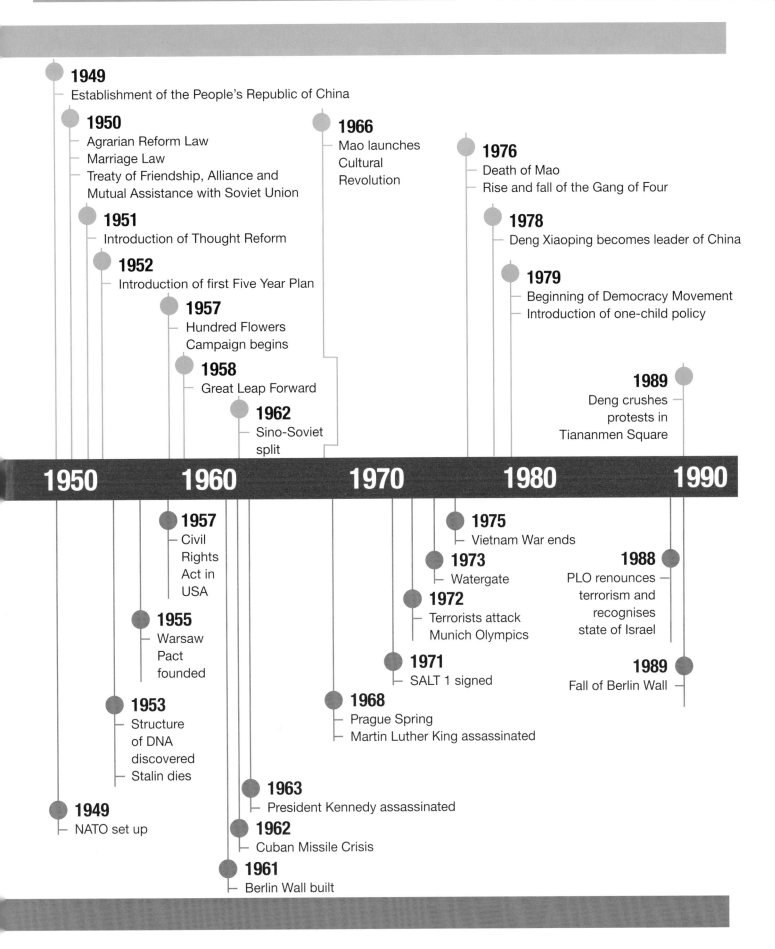

1949
Establishment of the People's Republic of China

1950
Agrarian Reform Law
Marriage Law
Treaty of Friendship, Alliance and
Mutual Assistance with Soviet Union

1951
Introduction of Thought Reform

1952
Introduction of first Five Year Plan

1957
Hundred Flowers
Campaign begins

1958
Great Leap Forward

1962
Sino-Soviet
split

1966
Mao launches
Cultural
Revolution

1976
Death of Mao
Rise and fall of the Gang of Four

1978
Deng Xiaoping becomes leader of China

1979
Beginning of Democracy Movement
Introduction of one-child policy

1989
Deng crushes
protests in
Tiananmen Square

1950   **1960**   **1970**   **1980**   **1990**

1957
Civil
Rights
Act in
USA

1955
Warsaw
Pact
founded

1953
Structure
of DNA
discovered
Stalin dies

1949
NATO set up

1963
President Kennedy assassinated

1962
Cuban Missile Crisis

1961
Berlin Wall built

1968
Prague Spring
Martin Luther King assassinated

1971
SALT 1 signed

1972
Terrorists attack
Munich Olympics

1973
Watergate

1975
Vietnam War ends

1988
PLO renounces
terrorism and
recognises
state of Israel

1989
Fall of Berlin Wall

1. THE FALL OF THE QING, WARLORDISM AND CHAOS, 1900–34

LEARNING OBJECTIVES

■ Understand the causes, events and consequences of the 1911 Revolution

■ Understand how China was ruled under the warlords

■ Understand the rise of the Guomindang and the Chinese Communist Party and the reasons for development of the United Front.

In 1900 the Qing imperial dynasty, which had been in power since 1644, ruled China. China was politically undeveloped; it was more like a medieval state than a 20th-century power. It was exploited for its economic resources by the Western powers and by its neighbour, Japan. In the period 1900–34, China experienced significant changes in its leadership and system of government. A revolution which overthrew the Qing dynasty and turned China into a republic prompted a period of great political trouble. In the absence of imperial rule, political power fell into the hands of warlords, who competed with one another for power. A nationalist party, the Guomindang, led first by Sun Yat-sen and later by Chiang Kai-shek, grew in strength and aimed to control China. At first it worked with the newly formed Chinese Communist Party in a United Front, but by 1934 the Guomindang and the Communists had become bitter enemies and were in conflict with one another.

1.1 CHINA IN THE EARLY 20TH CENTURY

LEARNING OBJECTIVES

■ Understand China at the beginning of the 20th century.

China is the largest country in Asia. At the beginning of the 20th century, it was the producer of many natural resources including tea, sugar, silk and opium. These resources could be moved around the country using China's natural rivers. Its wealth made it attractive to outside powers that increasingly came to China to exploit it. By the early 20th century, China was still one of the world's largest producers of manufactured goods, and its growing trade had enabled many cities to develop, such as Shanghai, which had become a major port for the import and export of goods.

RULING THE COUNTRY

China had been ruled by an emperor since 2000 BC. The emperor lived in the Forbidden City in Beijing and had the Mandate of Heaven. This meant that fate had given him the authority to rule and that his actions were seen as keeping within the natural laws of harmony. By 1900, the emperor ruled over a population of 300 million subjects who were divided into four main ethnic groups:

■ Han
■ Manchu
■ Mongol
■ Tibetan.

The Han formed 90 per cent of the population, but it was the Manchu that ruled. They had come from outside of China, from Manchuria in the north east. When the Manchu took control in China, they brought Manchuria into the empire. The development of the imperial system with its rules based on the works of the Chinese philosopher, Confucius, resulted in a strict class structure in China. An emperor who ruled with the Mandate of Heaven was not to be challenged by his subjects. Confucius taught that people should accept their position in society and obey orders. This philosophy supported the unquestioned authority of the emperor.

KEY TERM

imperial the rule of an emperor or empress over an empire

The business of government was conducted by a class called Mandarins, who were students of Confucius. They studied to pass examinations that allowed them advantages and rights, and then worked to prevent change.

The Mandarins had great advantages and rights, but most of the population were peasants and had few rights. The group with the least rights were women. They were the property of their fathers and husbands. Marriages were arranged and a 'bride-price' had to be paid. In many cases, women were bought and sold like cattle.

However, by the early 20th century, the emperor was beginning to lose the Mandate of Heaven. China was repeatedly humiliated by foreign powers who aimed to extend their power and wealth in China.

■ Britain had gained great wealth as a result of the opium trade and victory in the opium wars.
■ Japan had defeated China in war in 1894 and took control of Korea.
■ France had seized territory in the south.

These events revealed weaknesses in the power of the emperor, and his authority of the emperor had declined significantly.

▼ **Figure 1.1** Map of Imperial China in 1900

1.2 THE IMPACT OF THE BOXER UPRISING AND SELF-STRENGTHENING REFORM

LEARNING OBJECTIVES

- Understand the causes of the Boxer Uprising
- Understand the impact of the Boxer Uprising
- Understand self-strengthening and the reforms introduced in 1902–11.

The Qing **dynasty** that ruled China in 1900 came from Manchuria in north-east China, but most of the Chinese population came from the Han ethnic group. Manchuria originally lay outside China, so the Qing dynasty was seen as foreign to China. Most people resented the political domination of the Manchurians, but since Chinese culture encouraged respect for and acceptance of the political system, they remained obedient to it. The teachings of Confucius helped to keep the Qing emperors in power.

In the 19th century, the Qing had given rights to foreign powers to exploit China's economic resources. This increased the resentment towards the Imperial house and to foreigners. The Western powers not only brought their technology to change China's economy; they also brought **missionaries** to convert the Chinese from their traditional religious beliefs, which included **Confucianism** and **Buddhism**, to **Christianity**. Buddhism had been practised in China, particularly in Tibet, for over a thousand years. It taught that the way to end suffering in life was to achieve a state of **enlightenment**. Many Chinese people came to regard Westerners as foreign devils who had to be driven out if China was to be restored to greatness. This view was clearly seen in the Boxer Uprising (also known as the Boxer Rebellion), an attack on Westerners that broke out in 1899 in Shandong in northern China. The uprising spread to three of China's north-eastern **provinces** by 1900.

EXTEND YOUR KNOWLEDGE

The members of the Society of Righteous and Harmonious Fists were called 'Boxers' by Westerners. This was because they carried out exercises that they hoped would protect them from bullets and other forms of attack. The Westerners thought this looked like shadow boxing (fighting with an imaginary opponent).

THE CAUSES OF THE BOXER UPRISING

There were a number of factors that led to the uprising.
- In 1898, Emperor Guangxu tried to modernise the government and end the criticisms of the Qing dynasty and its policy of making **concessions** to foreigners. However, his policy of 'the Hundred Days Reform' was strongly opposed by his aunt, the **Empress Dowager** Cixi. She and her supporters seized control of the government and ended the reforms.
- The Chinese hatred of the 'foreign devils' included hatred of their religion as well as fear of their technology, especially the railways (which disturbed dragons) and the telegraph wires (which many Chinese people believed were poisonous). This hatred helped fuel attacks on foreigners.
- Cixi encouraged attacks on foreigners to avoid criticism of imperial rule.

EVENTS

By the late 1890s, a Chinese secret group, the Society of Righteous and Harmonious Fists (Boxers) began carrying out attacks on foreigners and Chinese Christians. The Boxers were mostly peasants, who had suffered from natural disasters such as famine and flooding, and believed the concessions

An image of the Boxer Uprising from a Paris journal printed in June 1900. The image shows the Boxers burning buildings and attacking telegraph wires.

KEY TERM

legation the headquarters of a foreign diplomatic minister and staff

given to foreigners made their lives even harder. The attacks began in Shandong and spread to Hebei, Shanxi and Henan in north-east China. The 'Boxers' attacked Christian missionaries, burned down their churches and schools, and killed both foreign and Chinese Christians. The uprising spread to Beijing, where the German ambassador was shot. The Western population retreated into the British **legation**, which was surrounded by Boxers for 55 days in a siege.

The Boxers had the support of Empress Dowager Cixi, who declared war on the foreigners, but they were unable to defeat the defences of the legation. The Westerners raised an international force which broke the siege. Many Boxers were executed in the streets by the international forces. Cixi and the emperor disguised themselves as peasants and fled south to Xian.

THE IMPACT OF THE BOXER UPRISING

From an account of the Boxer Uprising by Fei Qihao, a Chinese Christian and a teacher in a mission school.

The wicked chief of the province, Yü Hsien, announced that the foreign religions encouraged men to do evil. There were the Boxers who were faithful to their emperor, loyal to their country, and determined to work together to wipe out the foreign religion. Yü Hsien also offered to reward, either with titles or office or money, anyone who killed foreigners. When the leader of the province supported the Boxers, what could the men who worked below him do? It was a time of lawlessness, when not only Christians were killed, but hundreds of others whom individual Boxers resented.

Cixi's support for the Boxers was a great mistake. It hurt the authority of the Qing dynasty by showing the people that the imperial house was not able to free China from foreign control.

The immediate effect of the failure of the rebellion was a tightening of foreign control in China.

■ A severe financial penalty was put in place. The Western powers demanded £67 million in **reparations** to be paid over 39 years.
■ The Westerners insisted on the destruction of China's military fortifications and her arsenals of weapons.
■ Ten officials were executed.
■ Foreign soldiers were to be placed permanently in and around Beijing.

There were more wide-reaching consequences for the Qing rulers. In 1902, Cixi and the emperor were allowed to return to Beijing, but their authority had been severely damaged by the failure of the Boxer Uprising. In an attempt to save not just the reputation of the royal house, but also its very existence, Cixi, who was largely in control of the government, allowed a series of reforms to be started. However, the damage to the royal house from the failed Boxer Uprising was impossible to mend. The reforms Cixi introduced were too little and too late, and their failure to satisfy the reformers in China ultimately led to revolution in 1911 and the fall of the Qing dynasty.

SELF-STRENGTHENING AND REFORM 1902–11

In order to ensure the survival of the dynasty, Cixi began introducing reforms. Since her campaign against foreigners had failed in the uprising, she was now obliged to accept their presence in China and to make use of them. The reforms she introduced were inspired by the self-strengthening movement, which began in the 1860s. The purpose of self-strengthening was to learn from foreigners, to copy their sciences and technology, and to apply it in exploiting China's resources. Cixi believed that self-strengthening would re-establish China's power and save the Qing dynasty. Little had been achieved in the late 19th century. It was therefore now essential for the Qing that reforms should be introduced and that they should succeed.

▶ **Figure 1.2** A summary of reforms 1902–11

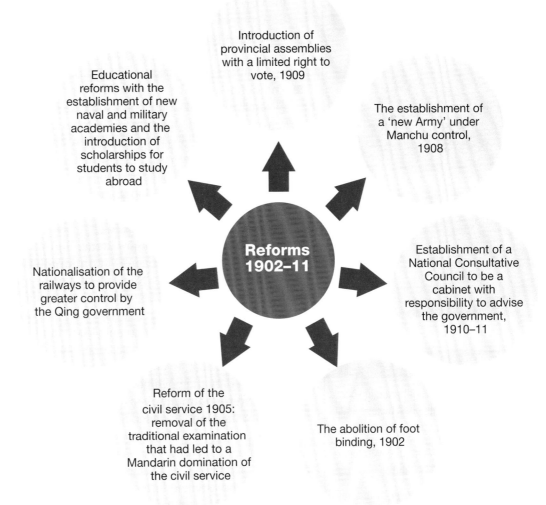

Introduction of provincial assemblies with a limited right to vote, 1909

Educational reforms with the establishment of new naval and military academies and the introduction of scholarships for students to study abroad

The establishment of a 'new Army' under Manchu control, 1908

Reforms 1902–11

Nationalisation of the railways to provide greater control by the Qing government

Establishment of a National Consultative Council to be a cabinet with responsibility to advise the government, 1910–11

Reform of the civil service 1905: removal of the traditional examination that had led to a Mandarin domination of the civil service

The abolition of foot binding, 1902

1.3 THE 1911 REVOLUTION

LEARNING OBJECTIVES

- Understand the causes of the 1911 Revolution
- Understand the key events of the 1911 Revolution
- Understand the results of the 1911 Revolution.

CAUSES

SOURCE C

The Emperor Puyi as a child in February 1910.

KEY TERMS

nationalism to take great pride in your country. Nationalists often believe that their country is superior to all others

republicanism a system of government with an elected head of state

nationalisation the takeover by the state of private companies and businesses

The power of the Qing dynasty was significantly reduced after the Boxer Uprising. A series of problems led to the revolution in 1911 which overthrew the dynasty.

- **Weak government:** In November 1908, both Emperor Guangxu and the Empress Cixi died. The new emperor, Puyi, was just 2 years old. Prince Chun, Guangxu's brother, ruled as **regent** and tried to save the dynasty by continuing with Cixi's reforms. However, Prince Chun was inexperienced in ruling and could not provide strong government.

- **The failure of the political reforms:** The reforms introduced in the years 1909–11 were too little and too late. The domination of the Manchus in the new National Consultative Council increased Han resentment of the government. The limits placed on the provincial assemblies (only 0.4 per cent of the population had the right to vote, and all changes were to be delayed for 9 years) led to calls for faster reform, and the failure of the government to do this increased support for revolution.

- **The consequences of the army reform:** The reform of the army was expensive and so Chun increased taxes on tea, wine, salt and land. These were on top of the taxes that had to be paid for the reparations owed after the Boxer Uprising. Furthermore, as part of the reforms, Prince Chun dismissed General Yuan Shikai who, he believed, was becoming too powerful. General Yuan declared he would get his revenge. These reforms were particularly damaging to the Qing dynasty, because the heavy taxes were unpopular with the ordinary people and the dismissal of Yuan created a powerful enemy to the **regime**.

- **The spread of revolutionary ideas:** Sun Yat-sen, who had been educated in the West, brought the ideas of **nationalism** and **republicanism** back to China (see pages 12–13). He was a great opponent of China's imperial government and believed that the Qing had to be **overthrown** in order for China to modernise. He was forced into exile in the years 1895–1911 because of his anti-government views, but this did not stop his ideas from spreading. They were especially popular among young Chinese men who travelled to Japan to complete their education, after scholarships were introduced by the government as part of educational reforms.

- **Growing resentment over the control of China's railways:** **Nationalisation** increased Manchu control in the provinces and the owners were angry that they did not receive full **compensation** for giving up ownership. This anger was increased when the Qing government paid for the expansion of railways by borrowing more money from the Western powers and granting further concessions to foreign companies to build the lines. It looked as if the Qing were partners with the 'foreign devils'. Growing anger among the population increased the possibility of revolution.

ACTIVITY

The reforms introduced in the years 1900–11 were intended to save the Qing dynasty.
Working with a partner, draw a table with two columns. On one side, list each of the reforms. On the other side, note down why each reform failed.

EXTEND YOUR KNOWLEDGE

The Emperor Guangxu died on 14 November 1908. It was suggested that the Empress Cixi had him poisoned by her favourite servant, because she was determined to live longer than him. The poisoning was confirmed in 2008 by forensic experts, who tested his remains and found high levels of the poison arsenic in his hair, stomach and burial clothes. However, if Cixi was responsible for the murder, she did not live long to enjoy her victory. The following day, it is said that she ate too many pears and fainted, and shortly afterwards she died.

EXAM-STYLE QUESTION

A01 **A02**

SKILLS ADAPTIVE LEARNING

Explain **two** causes of the 1911 Revolution in China. **(8 marks)**

HINT

This question is about causation. When explaining the reasons why something happened, you should identify two reasons, then use your knowledge to explain why those reasons caused the thing to happen. Write a detailed paragraph for each reason.

EVENTS

SOURCE D

An image from the 1911 Revolution. A Han soldier is shown cutting off a Manchu soldier's pigtail. The pigtail was a symbol of the superiority of the Manchu.

The revolution that overthrew the Qing began by accident. On 9 October 1911, a group of young revolutionaries in Hankou exploded a bomb that they were preparing for later use. Although this happened accidentally, it provided the signal for a wider revolt by those whose unhappiness with the Qing government now became revolutionary activity. The following day, known in China as the 'Double Tenth', soldiers in Wuhan began a **mutiny** which spread to other provinces until all but three provinces south of Beijing were in revolt. They declared themselves to be independent from government control. In particular, Han soldiers revolted against Manchu control and massacred Manchu troops. But the rebels lacked a leader. They found him in Yuan Shikai, the former general who wanted revenge for his dismissal in 1909. Although he had agreed to put down the rebellion for the government, when he reached Wuhan, he switched sides to support the rebels. He then returned to Beijing to form a Han government.

RESULTS

Sun Yat-sen was still in exile when the revolution began. In November he was offered the position of president, and he hurried back to China to take up his office on 1 January 1912. However, General Yuan persuaded Sun Yat-sen to step down and allow him to be president. In return, the general promised to persuade the Manchus to **abdicate** and to replace the imperial system with a **republic**. This was a significant concession because Yuan himself was not a republican. What he really wanted was to be the emperor.

An explanation of General Yuan Shikai's ambitions by a modern historian.

Yuan was in no sense a revolutionary; he was motivated as much by a dislike of republicanism as by his vendetta [hate campaign] against the Manchus who had humiliated him. He would allow the Manchu dynasty to fall but he had no intention of replacing it with a permanent republic. It was a matter of personal ambition. He saw in the situation an opportunity to use his military strength to lever [push] himself into power.

Sun stepped down because he did not have the military support to resist Yuan. Yuan's first act was to organise the abdication of 5-year-old Emperor Puyi. The abdication decree was issued on 12 February 1912.

SOURCE E

From the abdication decree issued on 12 February 1912.

I have induced [persuaded] the emperor to yield [give up] his authority to the country as a whole, determining [deciding] that there should be a constitutional republic. Yuan Shikai has full powers to organise a provisional [temporary] Republican government.

ACTIVITY

Write a paragraph to explain why Yuan Shikai became the leader of China in 1912.

1.4 CHINA UNDER THE WARLORDS, THE MAY THE FOURTH MOVEMENT AND THE RISE OF THE GUOMINDANG

LEARNING OBJECTIVES

- Understand how China was ruled during the warlord era
- Understand the May the Fourth Movement
- Understand the importance of Sun Yat-sen, Chiang Kai-shek and the rise of the Guomindang.

KEY TERM

Japan's Twenty-One Demands a set of demands imposed on China which gave Japan control over China's territory, forced China to appoint Japanese political and military advisers and buy weapons from Japan

With military support, from 1912 to 1916, Yuan Shikai ruled China as a **dictator**, and in 1915 he tried to make himself emperor. However, his rejection of democracy made him unpopular with Sun Yat-sen's new party, the Guomindang, and the military governors in the provinces feared that they would lose authority if Yuan took more power. The final crisis came when Yuan accepted most of **Japan's Twenty-One Demands** to control many of China's factories, railway lines and ports. The Twenty-One Demands were issued by Japan in 1915 to strengthen their position during the First World War. They would have resulted in a loss of China's independence. In December 1915, the army revolted against Yuan. He was forced to abandon his plan to become emperor. He died of a stroke in June 1916.

THE ERA OF THE WARLORDS, 1916–27

After Yuan's death, there was no military general who could rule China with the same authority. The central government collapsed, since although there was still technically a republican government in Beijing, in practice, power was exercised by powerful local generals in their own provinces. These generals were known as **warlords**. They ran their own legal and financial systems, collected taxes and terrorised their populations. Originally, most warlords took power because they were the military governors chosen by Yuan Shikai to manage the provinces. After 1920, some warlords were removed by other ambitious men who seized power. There were hundreds of warlords with different ideas and styles of ruling.

■ Feng Yuxiang was known as the 'Christian general'. He insisted on **baptising** his troops and believed that his province should be ruled by moral values. He carefully watched over the behaviour of his troops and refused to allow them to fight with one another.

■ Zang Zongzhang was a violent ruler who enjoyed splitting open the heads of his opponents; he called this 'splitting melons'.

■ Zhang Zuolin believed in the use of cruel punishments for his soldiers to warn them against attempting to mutiny. On one occasion he had two soldiers beheaded for entering a theatre without paying.

▶ **Figure 1.3** A map showing the major areas controlled by the warlords in the period 1916–27

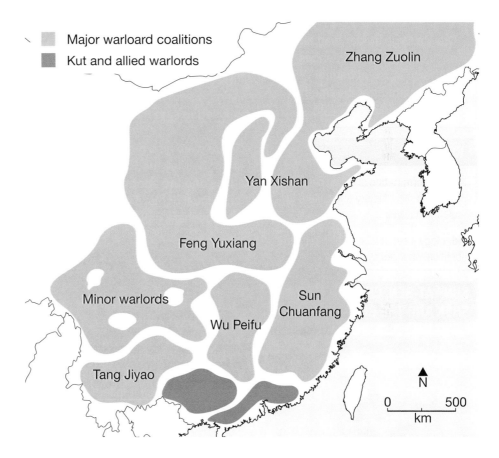

Although there were many differences among the warlords, they also had features in common.

■ None of them was prepared to give up their private armies or submit to an outside authority.

■ They were cruel rulers.

■ They made agreements with the foreign powers who wanted to protect their economic interests in China.

Warlord rule caused great suffering for the Chinese people. Not only were they treated with great cruelty, but when drought struck in 1918 and flooding in 1923–25, there was no effective central government to organise relief for the population. As a result, increasing numbers of Chinese people turned to revolutionary ideas.

EXAM-STYLE QUESTION

A01 **A02**

Explain **two** ways in which the way China was ruled in 1926 was different to how it was ruled in 1900. **(6 marks)**

> **HINT**
>
> This question is about comparison. You should identify two differences and give some details to explain in what way the features were different.

THE MAY THE FOURTH MOVEMENT, 1919

ACTIVITY

Draw a large spider diagram outlining the consequences of the collapse of central government after the death of Yuan Shikai.

KEY TERMS

self-determination allowing people of the same race, history and culture to rule themselves

ideology a set of ideas which refer to a political or social system

The May the Fourth Movement was driven by the news that Japan was to be given German possessions in the Shandong province under the terms of the Treaty of Versailles. This **treaty** had ended the First World War with Germany. In spite of discussions about **self-determination**, this concept was not applied to Germany or to China when her territory, previously ruled by Germany, was handed over to Japan. On 4 May 1919, students from Beijing University led a protest in Tiananmen Square. They called on the government to resist this humiliating treatment of China. The movement spread to other cities, where strikes and protests took place. As a result, China's government refused to sign the treaty.

There were also more significant consequences of the development of ideas from the May the Fourth Movement, including a rejection of old-fashioned ideas and the adoption of modern beliefs including freedom, democracy and equal rights. This was known as the New Tide. These ideas inspired revolutionary groups to fight to achieve unity and independence for China in the 1920s.

SUN YAT-SEN, CHIANG KAI-SHEK AND THE GUOMINDANG

SOURCE F

Dr Sun Yat-sen.

Sun Yat-sen was born in Guandong province in 1866. When he was 12 years old, he was sent to live with his elder brother who lived in Hawaii. Sun was educated in Honolulu, where he learned to speak English. Later on he moved to British-owned Hong Kong, where he studied medicine and converted to Christianity. Inspired by his **nationalist** beliefs, in 1895, he led a rebellion in Guangzou. When it failed, he was forced into exile. He travelled extensively in Europe, Japan, the USA and Canada, and returned to China after the 1911 Revolution, becoming president. However, after it had become clear that he could not fight against Yuan Shikai's military strength, he agreed to step down as president and fled to Japan, not returning to China until 1917.

When Sun returned to China in 1917, he set up his own nationalist government in Guangzhou. It was here that he declared the formation of the nationalist party, the Guomindang (GMD), in 1919. Sun announced the political **ideology** of the GMD in a speech in 1923. It was called the 'Three Principles of the People'. The Three Principles were a key moment in the growth of the GMD as a political party. They placed great emphasis on the people as a whole, rather than on the rights and freedoms of individuals. The main idea was to remove foreign control and then to raise up the Chinese people out of the poverty and old-fashioned world in which they lived.

The GMD needed to overthrow the warlords in order to take control of China. To do this, it needed an army. In 1924, Sun Yat-sen established the Whampoa

▼ **Figure 1.4** A summary of the 'Three Principles of the People'

National freedom
To remove foreigners and to restore China's nationalism

The Democracy Principle
The Chinese people to control their own government through elections

People's welfare
To solve the problem of poverty in China by developing government-owned industries and protecting native industry from foreign powers

Military Academy to train GMD soldiers, and the GMD became a military organisation. Its army was known as the New Republican Army (NRA).

Sun was assisted in his development of the GMD by advisers from the newly established **Bolshevik** government in Russia. Alfred Joffe organised negotiations and Mikhail Borodin helped to reorganise the GMD as a mass party with a powerful central leadership. Borodin also helped the GMD to acquire large quantities of arms for their campaign to destroy the warlords. It was Borodin who approved the appointment of Chiang Kai-shek as the commander of the GMD army. This was a key moment in the development of the GMD. When Sun Yat-sen died of cancer in 1925, Chiang was ideally placed to succeed him, and to lead the GMD's campaign to overthrow the warlords. This campaign became known as the Northern Expedition.

EXTEND YOUR KNOWLEDGE

In the modern spelling of Chinese names, the pin-yin system, Chiang Kai-shek is known as Jiang Jieshi. However, because the name Chiang Kai-shek is so familiar, most Western textbooks continue to use his name from the Giles-Wade system. The Giles-Wade system was developed in the 19th century and was based on a phonetic pronunciation of Chinese words.

KEY TERM

Bolshevik the communist government in Russia that had taken control after the 1917 Revolution in Russia

SOURCE G

Chiang Kai-shek in 1925 when he became leader of the GMD.

Originally, Chiang was not seen as the obvious replacement to Sun, because he was regarded as a military man and not a leader. However, this view underestimated his ambition and the importance of military power. Chiang himself was convinced that control of the army would give him control of China.

EXTRACT B

An explanation of Chiang Kai-shek's character and ambitions from a recent book on the history of China.

Chiang Kai-shek was seen as a military man with no claim to a big role in civilian government. Chiang was easy to underestimate. Known for his bad temper, he appeared to GMD leaders as a rough provincial type. But Chiang understood where power lay. 'If I control the army, I will have the power to control the country,' he told his wife. 'It is my road to leadership.'

ACTIVITY

Sun Yat-sen wanted to free China from foreign control. Why do you think he accepted help from the Soviet government in Russia? Working with a partner, list **two** advantages and **two** disadvantages of working with the Soviet government.

1.5 THE DEVELOPMENT OF THE UNITED FRONT

LEARNING OBJECTIVES

■ Understand how and why the Chinese Communist Party emerged and developed

■ Understand the establishment of the United Front and the Northern Expedition

■ Understand the reasons for the collapse of the United Front and the Extermination Campaign.

THE EMERGENCE OF THE CHINESE COMMUNIST PARTY

Stage 1: Primitive communism
In the Stone Age, all people were equal and shared the work according to their talents. They had an equal share of everything that was produced.

Stage 2: Feudalism
In the Middle Ages, all the land belonged to the King, who shared it with his lords. The majority of the people were peasants, who were exploited for their labour and owned by their lords.

Stage 3: Capitalism
In the 18th and 19th centuries, the increase in mechanised forms of production allowed a rich class of business owners – or capitalists, as Marx called them – to develop. Capitalists drew huge profits from the labour of their workers, called the proletariat. They paid their workers only a small fraction of the money made from their labour.

Stage 4: Communism
The exploitation of the workers under capitalism would lead them to rise up against the capitalists in a revolution. After the revolution, a state of equality would be achieved in which there were no classes and business, and all property was owned by the whole of society.

One consequence of the May the Fourth Movement was the spread of revolutionary ideas. One of these new ideas was communism. The German philosopher Karl Marx wrote about the theory of communism in the mid-19th century. Marx taught that history was a series of stages in which the **proletariat** struggled against the economic, political and social control of the higher classes. Eventually, through revolution, the higher classes would be overthrown and a state of equality would be achieved by the lower classes.

The table on the left gives a summary of Karl Marx's ideas, outlining the stages of history that would lead to revolution and the achievement of a **communist** system in which all people would be equal.

SOURCE H

A painting of Mao Zedong as he would have looked in 1921. Here Mao is on his way to lead a miners' strike. This painting was completed in 1967, when Mao was leader of China.

One of the reasons why communism was gaining in support was because there had been a successful communist revolution in Russia in 1917. China was very similar to Russia in that both countries were politically and economically old-fashioned. Chinese Communists believed that they could achieve a successful revolution in China.

The Chinese Communist Party (CCP) was founded in secret in a girls' school in Shanghai in June 1921. Chen Duxui, a key member of the May the Fourth Movement, was elected as the general-secretary. One of the 12 members invited to join the leadership of the party was a young bookseller from Hunan, Mao Zedong. He would later emerge as the leader of the CCP.

KEY TERM

proletariat the working classes who worked in factories and mines

THE INFLUENCE OF THE SOVIET UNION

The Bolshevik government in Russia wanted to encourage the spread of revolution and to protect its border with China. In the 1920s, it was convinced that the best way to achieve this was to work with the GMD.
- The CCP was too small to achieve revolution (it had only 50 members when it was founded).
- Conditions in China were not ready for a **Marxist** revolution. Karl Marx had taught that revolution would be led by the proletariat, but there were very few workers in China. The majority of the population were peasants.
- The GMD's 'Three Principles of the People' were rooted in ideas of equality and were therefore similar to communist ideas.

Therefore, the Soviet government in Russia, through its organisation the **Comintern**, encouraged the newly established CCP to work with the GMD to overthrow the warlords.

The CCP could not ignore the wishes of Russia, especially as it provided US$5000 a year to fund the party. Therefore, in 1923 the CCP agreed not only to co-operate with the GMD but also to become a group within it. Mao Zedong was one of those who followed party orders and joined the GMD.

KEY TERMS

Marxist relating to or based on Marxism, the system of political thinking invented by Karl Marx, which explains changes in history as the result of a struggle between social classes

Comintern the name of the Communist International organisation, established in 1919 to promote worldwide proletarian revolution

THE ESTABLISHMENT OF THE UNITED FRONT, 1924–27

The GMD and CCP had common aims that justified the establishment of the United Front, which were:
- to destroy the warlords
- to expel foreigners from China
- to improve the lives of ordinary Chinese people.

The decision to form a United Front was also encouraged by the 30 May Incident 1925. A protest by Chinese workers in Shanghai was stopped when the British commander from the **International Settlement** shot into the crowd and killed 12 people. This confirmed for the Nationalists and Communists that China's internal and external enemies could only be removed by force. Therefore, a United Front was formed. In 1926, Chiang called on its members to join in a battle to destroy the warlords. His speech launched the Northern Expedition.

KEY TERM

International Settlement in the 19th century foreigners lived in three places in Shanghai. By the early 20th century the American and British settlements merged to become the International Settlement. After the Boxer rebellion, Chinese people were forbidden to live in the International Settlement

EXAM-STYLE QUESTION

A01 | A02

SKILLS ADAPTIVE LEARNING

Explain **two** causes of the formation of the United Front in 1924–27. **(8 marks)**

HINT

This question is about causation. When answering questions on why something happened, good answers will clearly link the identified reasons for the outcome. Write an explanation for each of the factors, and link the reason to the formation of the United Front.

THE NORTHERN EXPEDITION, THE SHANGHAI MASSACRES AND THE EXTERMINATION CAMPAIGNS

THE NORTHERN EXPEDITION, 1926–28

The Northern Expedition was directed against the warlords in central, eastern and northern China. Its military strategy was to surround each individual warlord's army, to cut off its **supply lines** and to steadily destroy it. The New Republican Army (NRA) was very successful in achieving its objectives. With the help of its Soviet military adviser, Galen, the NRA had been built into a far more effective force than anything controlled by the warlord. He taught the NRA the value of surrounding the enemy's troops as a way of achieving victory. The troops were also taught to treat the local peasant populations with

SOURCE I

A Guomindang poster from 1926. Sun Yat-sen is shown at the top and Chiang Kai-shek is shown below on horseback, leading the GMD troops in the Northern Expedition.

respect, and were ordered to pay for food. In this way, they won the support of the local populations, who were tired of the bloody rule of the warlords. Mao Zedong played an important role in winning the support of local peasant populations for the United Front.

The strategy followed by the United Front led to fighting and many injuries, but it also brought success. By the summer of 1927, the United Front had taken control of central China and by 1928, with an army that numbered 250,000 men, Chiang took control of eastern China. The final stage came in April 1928, when Chiang drove the warlord Zhang Zuolin out of Beijing in the north. He then declared that the GMD was the legal government in China, and moved the capital city from Beijing in the north to Nanjing in the east.

Reasons for the victory of the United Front include:
- the strength and tactics of the United Front army compared to the private armies of the warlords
- the role of the Communists in gaining the support of the peasants for the United Front
- deals made by Chiang with the warlords – Chiang bribed individual warlords and allowed them to keep their private armies if they submitted to the control of the GMD.

Even before the campaign had brought victory, Chiang had become convinced that the United Front had succeeded in defeating the warlords and it had therefore served its purpose. Chiang had been suspicious of the Communists even before the Northern Expedition began. Chiang was from the rich classes in China, and the GMD relied on businessmen for financial support. They would never accept the ideology of communism and its aim to overthrow capitalism. The crisis between the GMD and CCP came in March 1927. The GMD were able to occupy Shanghai because the Communists had organised a general strike and left-wing uprisings that weakened the control of the city. The next month, Chiang arranged to destroy the Communists in Shanghai.

THE SHANGHAI MASSACRES, 1927

The GMD were able to take control of Shanghai because of the work of its left-wing members and the Communists, who had built a strong trade union organisation in the city. However, 2 weeks after taking control, Chiang turned on the Communists. He was supported by Shanghai's industrialists and traders, who opposed trade unions, and by the foreigners in the International Settlement, who were afraid that they would lose their economic interests if the Communists took control. Chiang's troops began a frenzy of killing which has been called the 'White Terror', a term used to describe nationalists and to distinguish them from the Communists or 'Reds'. They were supported by the violent secret societies (triads) in Shanghai and the crime organisation known as the Green Gang. More than 5,000 Communists were dragged out and killed. The attacks spread to other areas. In Hunan, more than a quarter of a million people were killed.

Mao and the Communists did not follow orders from the Comintern to continue the United Front at any cost and staged the Autumn Harvest Uprising in August–September 1927. However, their army was too small to take on the might of the NRA. Mao and his followers were forced to flee to the mountains of Jiangxi province. Here they set up a 'Chinese Soviet Republic', generally known as the Jiangxi **Soviet**, to govern the province. They spent the next 7 years in a struggle for survival there.

KEY TERM

soviet a communist council

SOURCE J

The massacre of Communists in Shanghai, whose leaders were captured and beheaded by government troops.

THE EXTERMINATION CAMPAIGNS, 1930–34

Chiang was determined to destroy the Communists. He believed that they were an even greater threat than the warlords. In the years 1930–34, he launched five extermination campaigns. The first was launched in October 1930, with 44,000 NRA troops directed at the Communists in Jiangxi. Chiang intended to surround and destroy the Communists. However, his plan failed completely. The Communists refused to fight face to face with the GMD, and instead tricked the NRA in order to enter their territory and then laid traps for them.

The Communists captured the commander of the first army unit and tortured him, cutting out his tongue and damaging his face before they beheaded him. Chiang took personal direction of the next campaign, directing 100,000 troops against the CCP in July 1931. However, even though he caught the Reds by surprise, his cautious strategy of moving slowly to avoid ambushes allowed the much smaller communist forces to escape. Chiang's troops met with opposition from the peasants, had too little to eat and caught dysentery from the dirty water. The troops reacted violently by burning down villages, massacring all the inhabitants and seizing their crops. Lack of support from the peasants was a key reason why Chiang's extermination campaign did not succeed. Chiang attempted to recruit volunteers from the villages to help find the Communists, but villagers were unwilling, as they were unhappy with the violent actions of the GMD.

More than a million peasants were killed by the GMD in the years 1930–34. However, the larger numbers of the GMD did begin to wear down the communist forces. In autumn 1933, the GMD launched its fifth and final extermination campaign. The Nationalists established a blockade around the soviet and deprived the inhabitants of food. They built over 11,000 km of roads into the soviet to allow the faster movement of troops. Chiang's new military adviser, the German General Hans von Seeckt, advised the building of defences to force the Communists back and to provide shelter for the NRA. This allowed the GMD to surround the Communists and the **scorched earth policy** used by the Nationalists also meant that the Reds would have no alternative but to fight a static war. The Reds faced defeat after defeat; by October 1934 they were left with no alternative but to abandon the Jiangxi Soviet. They had lost over 60,000 soldiers and more than half of their territory.

KEY TERM

scorched earth policy the tactic of destroying everything that might be useful to an army in an area, including buildings and crops in the fields

ACTIVITY

Working with a partner, decide who will represent a member of the GMD and who will represent the CCP. Write a diary entry to describe your involvement in the United Front, the Northern Expedition and the Shanghai Massacres. Compare your descriptions. In what ways are they the same? How do they differ?

RECAP

RECALL QUESTIONS

1 What was the name of the imperial dynasty ruling China in 1900?
2 Which group of people did the Boxers attack in the 1900 Uprising?
3 Who became the leader of the government after the 1911 Revolution?
4 Why was Feng Yuxiang known as the Christian general?
5 What were the main ideas in Sun Yat-sen's Three Principles of the People?
6 What was the name of the GMD army?
7 Where was the Chinese Communist Party founded?
8 What was the aim of the United Front?
9 Who played an important role in winning the support of the peasants for the United Front?
10 What is the name given to the massacre of Communists by the GMD?

CHECKPOINT

STRENGTHEN
S1 Write a paragraph describing the events of the Boxer Uprising.
S2 Who was Sun Yat-sen, and why was he important?
S3 List three reasons why the Northern Expedition was successful in overthrowing the warlords.

CHALLENGE
C1 What were the main consequences of the Boxer Uprising?
C2 Compare the ideas of the GMD and the CCP. Draw up a table with two columns: one for the GMD and one for the CCP. List their ideas. Highlight the points that are similar.
C3 In what ways did the government of China change in the years 1900–34? Draw up a timeline of the years and plot the different governments on it. Use it to help you write a short paragraph describing the changes.

SUMMARY

■ Resentment against foreign control led to the Boxer Uprising in 1900.
■ The failure of reform in the years 1902–11 led to the outbreak of revolution in 1911, the fall of the Qing dynasty and the declaration of a republic in 1912.
■ China's new republic soon dissolved into chaos as warlords seized control in the provinces and ruled with private armies.
■ The spread of revolutionary ideas encouraged the growth of nationalism, the development of the Guomindang under Sun Yat-sen and the birth of the Chinese Communist Party.
■ Under the influence of advisers from the Soviet Union, the GMD and CCP formed a United Front to defeat the warlords.
■ The United Front defeated the warlords in the Northern Expedition of 1926–28 and established a GMD government in Nanjing in 1928.
■ Under the orders of Chiang Kai-shek, the GMD turned against the Communists and massacred thousands in Shanghai and in the following extermination campaigns.
■ The Communists were forced to flee to Jianxi in order to survive.

EXAM GUIDANCE: PART (A) QUESTIONS

A01 **A02**

Question to be answered: Explain two ways in which the way China was ruled by the Qing dynasty in the years 1900–11 was similar to the way it was ruled in the warlord era (1916–27).   (6 marks)

1 **Analysis Question 1: What is the question type testing?**
In this question, you have to demonstrate that you have knowledge and understanding of the key features and characteristics of the period studied. In this particular case, it is knowledge and understanding of how China was ruled at the beginning of the 20th century.

You also have to explain, analyse and make judgements about historical events and periods to explain ways in which there were similarities between those events/periods.

2 **Analysis Question 2: What do I have to do to answer the question well?**
Obviously you have to write about the Qing dynasty and the warlord era, but this is not just a case of writing everything you know. You have to identify two similarities and provide details showing how the two ways of ruling China were similar. If you just write about events under the two governments, you are unlikely to do this. So you should start by identifying ways in which they are similar and then give details to prove it. For example, if you were allowed to put sub-headings in your answers, the two similarities would be the two sub-headings you would use.

So in this case, you might consider the way that they ruled and the ways that they treated the people. You will get one mark for the similarity you show, one mark for explaining that similarity and another mark for detail.

3 **Analysis Question 3: Are there any techniques I can use to make it very clear that I am doing what is needed to be successful?**
This is a 6-mark question and you need to make sure you leave enough time to answer the other two questions fully (they are worth 24 marks in total). Therefore, you need to get straight in to writing your answer. The question asks for two similarities, so it is a good idea to write two paragraphs and to begin each paragraph with phrases like 'One similarity was…' and 'Another similarity was…'. You will get a maximum of 3 marks for each similarity you explain, so make sure you do two similarities.

N.B The question does not ask 'How similar', so you do not have to point out similarities and differences. You should just focus on similarities.

Answer A

In the years 1900–1911, the Qing dynasty was a weak government and in 1911 it was overthrown by a revolution. The warlords who were also weak and were overthrown by the Northern Expedition. A second similarity is that they treated the people harshly.

What are the strengths and weaknesses of Answer A?

This answer has some merits. It identifies a similarity (both types of government were weak) and gives some support to the idea that both governments were overthrown – but it does not support the similarity that they treated the people harshly and does not develop the similarity on weak government. It is unlikely that this answer would score more than two or three marks.

Answer B

One similarity is that both the types of government were very weak. The Qing dynasty was very weak after it had to pay the Western powers £67 million in reparations after the Boxer Rebellion. It was too weak to stop revolutionary ideas spreading and this led to its overthrow in the 1911 Revolution. This was very similar to the rule of the warlords. The warlords were very weak because they each only controlled a small area of China and they could not deal with problems in China like drought and famine. They could not stop the spread of revolutionary ideas, like nationalism and communism.

A second similarity was that both the Qing dynasty and the warlords treated the ordinary people very harshly. The Qing put really high taxes on goods like tea and salt which made it difficult for the Chinese people to afford basic foods. The warlords were also harsh. One warlord called Zang Zongzhang used to split open the heads of his opponents.

What are the strengths and weaknesses of Answer B?

This is an excellent answer. Each paragraph begins by giving a similarity and goes on to provide factual support to explain that similarity. It would be likely to receive full marks.

Challenge a friend

Use the Student Book to set a part (a) question for a friend. Then look at the answer. Does it do the following things?

☐ Provide two similarities
☐ Provide detailed information to explain why they are similarities.

If it does, you can tell your friend that the answer is very good!

2. THE TRIUMPH OF MAO AND THE CCP, 1934–49

LEARNING OBJECTIVES

■ Understand the events and the importance of the Long March

■ Understand the role of the CCP and the Red Army in the war against Japan

■ Understand the reasons for the Civil War, its key features and why the CCP was successful.

In 1934, under siege by the Guomindang (GMD) and with survival very unlikely, the Communists broke out of the Jiangxi Soviet in search for a new base where they would be safe from attack. The result was the Long March. For more than a year, the Communists battled with the GMD until they reached Yanan in northern China. Here they built their base and Mao developed his ideas about Chinese communism. During this period China was invaded and occupied by the Japanese. Chiang Kai-shek was unable to resist the Japanese using the GMD forces alone, and so from 1937–45 the Chinese Communist Party (CCP) and the GMD formed a second United Front to remove the Japanese. However, as soon as this was achieved, the United Front broke up once again, and from 1945 to 1949 a bloody civil war was fought between the CCP and the GMD for control of China. By 1949, the Communists had won the civil war and on 1 October 1949, Mao Zedong, leader of the CCP, declared that China was a communist Republic.

2.1 THE EVENTS AND IMPORTANCE OF THE LONG MARCH, 1934–35

LEARNING OBJECTIVES

- Understand the reasons why the Communists began the Long March
- Understand the events of the Long March
- Understand the importance of the Long March.

THE JIANGXI SOVIET AND THE GMD ENCIRCLEMENT CAMPAIGNS, 1927–34

When Chiang launched the White Terror, the Communists hid in the Jingang Mountains. There they organised the Jiangxi Soviet. It was here that Mao developed his version of communism that relied on the peasants as the force for revolution. He strongly disagreed with the Comintern advisers who stuck closely to the teaching of Karl Marx that revolution would be led by the proletariat. However, Mao insisted on concentrating on winning the support of the peasants. This put him in a good position in the struggle for the leadership of the party later on.

KEY TERM

Reds a term used to describe the parties of the political left-wing, socialists and communists. Red is the colour associated with revolution

Although the establishment of the Jiangxi Soviet was successful, the constant attacks by the GMD threatened it. Chiang was advised by his new German military advisers to surround the **Reds**, and push them into a smaller and smaller area so that they lost all access to resources. The GMD could then use aerial bombing to attack the enclosed communist forces. By October 1934, it was clear that Chiang's approach meant the Communists could not survive if they remained in the Jiangxi Soviet. Therefore, on the night of 16 October, 80,000–100,000 Communists broke out of the Jiangxi Soviet and began to march north to find a place of safety. This became known as the Long March.

EXAM-STYLE QUESTION

A01 **A02**

SKILLS ADAPTIVE LEARNING

Explain **two** causes of the Long March.   (8 marks)

> **HINT**
>
> This question is about causation. When explaining the reasons why something happened, you should identify two reasons, and write a paragraph for each reason to explain how it led to the outcome.

THE EVENTS OF THE LONG MARCH

When the Communists began their march, they had no idea where their destination would be. They were followed all the way by the GMD army and fought battle after battle before they finally escaped the GMD and found safety in Yanan. At first, the Communists were led by the Comintern adviser Otto Braun. He encouraged the Red Army to fight with the GMD forces in urban areas. However, this led to heavy losses.

After the meeting at Zunyi in January 1935, Mao Zedong and Zhu De, a former warlord who had become a Communist, took control of the party. They developed new tactic which led the Red Army in a series of surprising directions and involved dividing the forces and regrouping in order to escape from the GMD. The route north took them across mountains, rivers and

▶ **Figure 2.1** Map of the Long March showing the route from the Jiangxi Soviet to Yanan

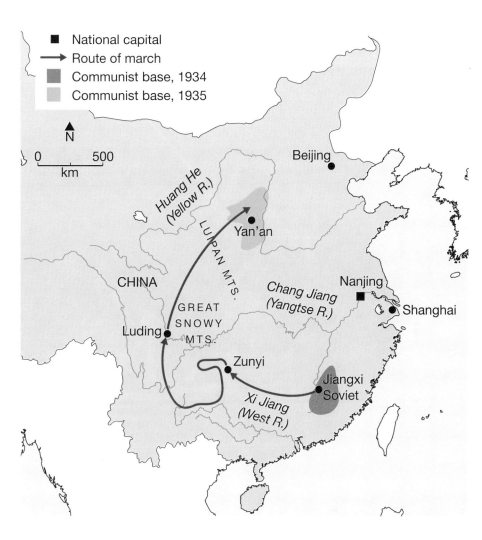

- ■ National capital
- → Route of march
- Communist base, 1934
- Communist base, 1935

General Zhu De of the Red Army speaking to his troops during the Long March.

deserts. In May 1935, the marchers crossed the Yangtze River and then the Dadu River, where 22 soldiers were said to have swung across the river on chains while the enemy shot at them.

The events of the Long March have since become a tale of outstanding bravery and success. The conditions were extreme. The troops crossed lands where the water was unfit to drink and thousands died of hunger, drowned or froze to death. When they arrived in Yanan in northern China in October 1935, only 10,000 of the original 80,000 marchers had survived.

EXTEND YOUR KNOWLEDGE

The most difficult part of the Long March was when the marchers crossed the icy marshlands on route to Gansu in the north-east. They had to cross a freezing marshland. There was little food, and many of the marchers suffered with diarrhoea and died. Some were only able to survive by picking out grains from the bloody faeces of their dying companions.

Chinese communist troops crossing the Dadu River after fighting Nationalist forces during the Long March.

THE IMPORTANCE OF THE LONG MARCH

The Long March was turned into a brave myth of survival by the CCP. In reality, it began as an act of desperation as the Communists were forced out of their southern base by the GMD, and by the end only a very small number of the marchers survived the experience. Instead of calling it the Long March, the GMD always referred to it as the Great Retreat. Of the 80,000 marchers who set out from Jiangxi, only 10,000 made it to Yanan, and it was not even certain that they were safe there. In the meantime, Chiang Kai-shek's government was officially recognised by the West and the Soviet Union, and it looked as if Nationalist control of China was secure.

However, there were also positive achievements. The Long March provided excellent **propaganda** and created **martyrs** for the communist cause. It promoted the idea of **comradeship** and self-sacrifice, which were to remain key features of Chinese communism. It encouraged support for the Red Army from the peasants who had been treated well by the soldiers. Furthermore, it established Mao as the leader and allowed the CCP to develop the theory of communism in practice at their new base in Yanan, where they were to remain for the next 10 years.

Figure 2.2 summarises the importance of the Long March.

► **Figure 2.2** A summary of the positive and negative results of the Long March

Positive

The Long March promoted the idea of comradeship and self-sacrifice for the cause.

The Long March was excellent propaganda and provided martyrs to promote the communist cause.

The Communists were able to establish a new base at Yanan, where they developed the theory of Chinese Communism in practice for the next 12 years.

Mao's position as leader was confirmed. Other leading Communists (Zhu De, Zhou Enlai and Liu Shaoqi) were all veterans of the Long March.

The Red Army won the support of peasants as they marched through villages.

Only about 10,000 out of 80,000 of the marchers survived.

There was no certainty that the Yanan Soviet would survive.

Nationalist control of China seemed to be certain. Chiang's government was recognised by the West and the Soviet Union, while the CCP struggled to survive.

GMD accounts of the event called it the Great Retreat.

Negative

Figure 2.2 A summary of the positive and negative results of the Long March

---

EXTRACT A

An account of part of the Long March by a Chinese historian.

The conditions under which the Long March began could not have been worse, with totally inadequate food supplies, heavy baggage and no battle plans. Li Teh was in charge of our escape from the Kuomintang.

It appears that all that Li Teh knew of military science was the straight, straight line. He drew a straight line and that was the line of our march. But one important detail had been forgotten. Maps. There were no maps except the maps Mao had collected. The Red Army men, exhausted after months of combat, of malnutrition, lack of salt, and fighting had not had time to rest. Yet these incredible peasants and workers pressed on and nine battles were fought against 100 regiments of the Kuomintang; 25,000 Red Army men died in the breakthrough.

Read Extract A.
1 Make a list of all the difficulties that the Red Army faced on this march.
2 Why do you think they kept going in such terrible conditions?

During the first ten days the orders were to walk by night and rest by day; but there was no rest, as they were constantly attacked. The orders were changed to four hours of marching and four hours rest, day and night. But again there was no rest, for they were attacked, had no time to eat, to find shelter, water, before they were on the march again.

'We were so tired, we strapped ourselves to trees, to our guns, we strung ourselves to each other. We slept standing up, we slept walking. Long rows of us roped ourselves together so as to keep on the march. We called it sleep flying.'

Always going straight as a ruler, the Red Army arrived on the east bank of the Hsiang river. It had to be crossed, but a vast Kuomintang force barred the way. The Red Army waded through, the tall carrying the short; the children of 12 and 13 who in their hundreds had come to the Army and served as orderlies, cookboys, carriers and trumpeters sat on the veterans' shoulders.

The battle to cross the Hsiang river lasted a week, with horrifying losses. The dead and the dying littered the bank. It cost another 30,000 men. They had to leave some of the wounded behind, there was no way to carry them. By now half of the troops that had set off had been either killed or wounded. But the 'Head on, straight on' Li Teh would not change the orders.

2.2 WAR WITH JAPAN, 1937–45

LEARNING OBJECTIVES

■ Understand the reasons for the war with Japan

■ Understand the reasons for the formation of a second United Front

■ Understand the events of the war with Japan and the roles played by the GMD and CCP.

Japan had a long history of wanting to win Chinese territory. In the late 19th and early 20th centuries, Japan had modernised its economy and military and become a very strong power, as shown by its defeat of China in 1895 and of Russia in 1905. During the 1920s, Japan's economic growth began to slow down because it could not get the raw materials, such as oil, that it needed to expand. Japan had ambitions to expand its territory into China, which had the raw material that Japan needed. In 1931, Japan invaded Manchuria and turned it into a puppet state. Manchuria appeared to be independent but was in fact controlled by Japan, with the last Qing emperor, Puyi, as its puppet-ruler. In 1932, the Japanese renamed the province Manchukuo. From this base, they moved to Shanghai, which was forced to submit to them.

EXTEND YOUR KNOWLEDGE

The former emperor Puyi wanted to be emperor again. In 1932, after the Japanese invasion of Manchuria, he travelled to the province and was installed as emperor of Manghuguo. However, he was angry with the Japanese because the Qing dynasty had not been restored. He returned to China after Mao's victory in 1949. He served 10 years in a war criminals' centre, and after giving support to the communist government, he lived the rest of his life as an ordinary citizen. Puyi died in October 1967. His life was the subject of the film *The Last Emperor*.

In the years 1931–37, the Japanese strengthened their position in China in the areas that they had occupied. From 1937, they began to expand into new territories. Chiang Kai-shek's initial response had been to allow the Japanese to take the land. He was convinced that they could never occupy a country as large as China. However, this approach had made him unpopular with the Chinese population and could not be continued once the Japanese began a full-scale occupation policy. Therefore, in July 1937, Chiang declared that China was at war with Japan (see Figure 2.3).

▶ **Figure 2.3** Map of the Sino–Japanese War, 1937–45

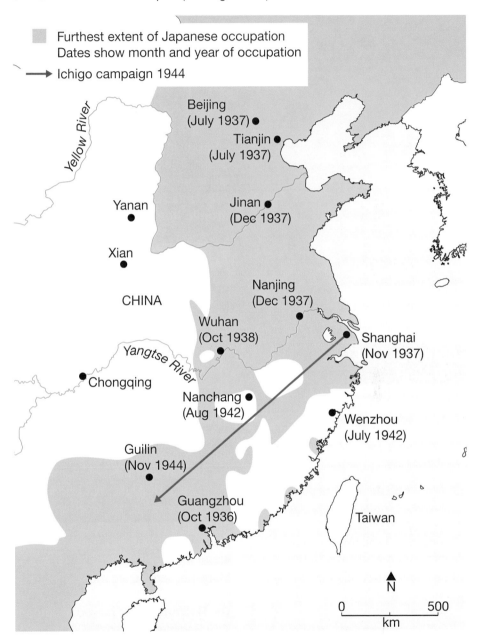

THE FORMATION OF A SECOND UNITED FRONT

Chiang considered that the Communists were a greater threat to China than the Japanese, and had therefore accepted the Japanese occupation of Manchuria and the northern provinces. However, China was difficult to govern. Chiang had relied on deals with the warlords to keep control of the country. They wanted Chiang to focus on removing the Japanese rather than on fighting with the Communists. In December 1936, they put pressure on to Chiang to work with the Communists to force the Japanese out of China.

THE EVENTS IN THE WAR AGAINST JAPAN, 1937–45

SOURCE C

The stream of Chinese refugees fleeing after the Japanese capture of the port of Shanghai in 1937.

As a consequence, a second United Front between the GMD and the CCP was created. Although they would fight as separate armies, they did have a common goal: the removal of Japan from China.

The first 4 years of the war went badly for China. The Japanese captured major cities, including Shanghai, Beijing and the GMD capital of Nanjing, forcing Chiang's government to flee to Chongqing. The Chinese people also suffered extreme violence from the Japanese troops. In the 'rape of Nanjing' in December 1937, over 30,000 Chinese were killed and 20,000 women and girls were repeatedly raped by gangs of soldiers. The Japanese even persuaded a former colleague of Chiang's, Wang Jingwei, to become the leader of the 'New Government of China' for the Japanese. It looked as if China would be defeated.

China's fortunes changed in 1941, after the Japanese bombing of Pearl Harbor in December of that year. After this event, the Allies, the USA, the Soviet Union and Britain supplied China with resources and funding to help them defeat Japan. The Soviet Union sent planes with Soviet pilots. Although Chiang was still more concerned about the Communists than the Japanese, by 1945, the Allied attacks on the Japanese mainland weakened the Japanese. The two **atomic bombs** dropped in August 1945 ended the war.

EXTEND YOUR KNOWLEDGE

The Japanese bombed Pearl Harbor on 7 December 1941. Japan wanted to warn America that it was not to interfere with Japan's plans to build an empire in South-east Asia. In fact, the action led to America joining the Second World War.

THE ROLE OF THE CCP AND THE RED ARMY

SOURCE D

Mao's orders to the Red Army on how to treat the peasants.

1 Replace all doors when you leave a house. [*Doors in peasant homes were on hooks.*]

2 Return and roll up the grass matting on which you sleep.

3 Be considerate and polite to the people and help them when you can.

4 Return all borrowed articles.

5 Replace all damaged articles.

6 Be honest in all dealings with the peasants.

7 Pay for all articles purchased.

8 Be clean and especially, establish toilets a safe distance from people's houses.

The Allies recognised Chiang as the leader of China, and the CCP entered into the United Front with the clear knowledge that Chiang was in control. However, the CCP was a powerful force in the war. The party membership expanded rapidly during the war so that by 1945 it had grown from 40,000 in 1937 to 1.2 million. Much of this increase can be explained by the popular policies that Mao implemented in the Yanan Soviet. He not only won over the peasants by insisting that the Red Army treat them with respect when they entered villages, but also insisted that landlords should not be seen as the enemy. He had won them over by applying rent controls rather than trying to wipe them out as a class enemy. The support of the peasants for the Communists was very important during the war. They informed the Red Army about the position of the Japanese, and provided it with food and shelter. Many peasants were recruited into the Red Army.

The Red Army itself played an important role in the war against Japan. The '100 Regiments Offensive', launched in 1940, was one of the Red Army's first successes. Communist forces numbering over 400,000 attacked the Japanese in northern and central China, where they captured Japanese soldiers and destroyed over 965 km of railway lines. Although the Japanese were strong enough to launch a counter-campaign and push the Red Army back, the Communists had demonstrated that they were eager to remove the Japanese from China, and this further increased their support. In comparison to Chiang and the GMD, the Communists appeared to be much more determined to defeat Japan.

SOURCE E

An assessment of the role of the Communist in the war against Japan by Mao Zedong in a speech he made at Yanan on 13 August 1945.

During the past eight years, the people of our areas, receiving no help from outside and relying entirely on their own efforts, freed vast territories and pinned down the majority of the Japanese invading forces. Only by our determined resistance and brave struggle were the 200 million people in our areas saved from being crushed by Japanese invaders. Chiang hid in Chongqing with guards in front of him.

The Red Army used **guerrilla tactics** against the Japanese; they ambushed Japanese forces, attacked the weak points in their defences and prevented them from moving forwards. This was much more successful than fighting pitched battles in the cities, where the Japanese could more easily identify the enemy. At the end of the war, Mao claimed that his strategy had been a great success and that the Communists had saved China from Japan. His claims were clearly propaganda, for without the help of the Allies and the use of the atomic bomb, the war in China would not have ended in 1945. However, his strategy did help to attract more support to the communist cause.

ACTIVITY

Read Source E. It is very favourable towards the Communists. Rewrite it from a neutral point of view.

THE LIMITATIONS OF THE GUOMINDANG

KEY TERM

guerrilla tactics a type of fighting using ambushes and attacks to fight a larger, less mobile army. The key feature is the element of surprise in carrying out the attack

The performance of the GMD forces in the war was poor. One of the key problems was that Chiang persisted in seeing the Communists as the real enemy. For example, in January 1941, Chiang ordered his forces to attack the Communists in south China in spite of the co-operation promised in the United Front. The American Chief of Staff for South-east Asia, Joseph Stillwell, said that Chiang wasted resources supplied for the war by continuing to quarrel with the Communists. In 1944, the Japanese launched a new offensive. However, Chiang would not direct his army against the Japanese, as the Americans requested, because he was using it to besiege the Communists in Yanan.

Overall, the performance of the GMD was poor, both in terms of its military performance and its leadership of China:
- The GMD areas suffered from heavy bombing; Chongqing was the most heavily bombed city in the 20th century.
- The GMD guerrilla warfare had little impact on the Japanese army.
- The GMD army often lacked the will to fight and tended to break down when put under pressure.
- The GMD forces were recruited by force and discipline was tough, which meant that they lacked loyalty to the GMD cause.
- The GMD government, firstly in Nanjing and later in Chongqing, was dishonest.
- The GMD was unpopular with the peasants. GMD economic policies imposed high taxes and allowed some individuals to get richer through storing up goods for their own personal use and then buying and selling goods on the black market, while the majority suffered.
- The GMD was also unpopular with the peasants because of the way the peasants were treated by the GMD forces and the methods used to conscript them into the GMD army.

EXAM-STYLE QUESTION

A01 A02

Explain **two** ways in which the position of the CCP in 1945 was different to its position in 1921.
(6 marks)

HINT

This question is about comparison. You should identify two differences and give some details to explain in what way the features were different.

Mao Zedong and Chiang Kai-shek celebrating the defeat of Japan in 1945.

2.3 KEY FEATURES OF THE CIVIL WAR, 1946–49

LEARNING OBJECTIVES

- Understand the reasons for the outbreak of civil war between the GMD and the Communists
- Understand the key features of the Civil War
- Understand the importance of the Battle of Huai-Hai.

THE OUTBREAK OF THE CIVIL WAR

KEY TERM

civil war a conflict by two opposing sides in the same country

EXTEND YOUR KNOWLEDGE

Almost as soon as the Second World War ended, a new type of conflict emerged known as the Cold War. This was a conflict between the capitalist countries in the west led by the USA, and the communist countries in the east led by the Soviet Union. The two sides struggled for dominance, and built nuclear weapons to deter their enemy from attacking them. China, as a communist country, was supported by the Soviet Union.

The dropping of the atomic bombs on Japan ended the Second World War suddenly, before either the GMD or the CCP were ready to take control of China. Chiang had always put the destruction of the Reds as his priority, but he had not achieved this when the war ended. **Civil war** was impossible to avoid, but neither side was prepared to start it. The Nationalists held a large area in southern and central China, and the Communists controlled the countryside in northern and north-eastern China from their base in Yanan. As the Japanese retreated from the occupied territories in north and central China, both sides tried to occupy as much territory as they could. This was further complicated by the Soviet Union, which sent its Red Army into Manchuria in August 1945, trying to take control of that region.

Chiang was in the stronger position. The GMD was recognised as the real government in China, and the Americans insisted that the Japanese admit defeat to the GMD. The Americans persuaded both the Nationalists and the Communists to agree to stop fighting. They were worried that the Soviet Union might exploit the divisions in China and expand their control into the region. However, when Chiang tried to set up a new government which gave almost total power to the GMD, the Communists left the talks. Fighting occurred again, and by December 1945, both sides were at war. It is hard to put a date on the outbreak of the Civil War; unlike in a war between two countries, no official declaration of war was made. However, by July 1946, it was clear that there was no chance of a negotiated agreement, and a major struggle for the control of China had begun.

KEY STAGES IN THE CIVIL WAR

The Civil War can be divided into three main stages.

In the first stage, between July 1946 and May 1947, the GMD was initially successful. It captured a number of large cities in the north and established a route through to Manchuria. It was so successful that the Communists lost control of Yanan. However, the communist army, now renamed the People's Liberation Army (PLA), developed successful guerrilla tactics and by May 1947, it had secured control of northern Manchuria. This significantly strengthened the Communists.

The second stage of the conflict occurred between May 1947 and November 1948. The PLA launched full-scale attacks on the GMD and switched to **conventional warfare**; the army pushed into central and western China, although it continued to enjoy victories in Manchuria in the north. The GMD became increasingly cut-off from the rest of China in its shrinking territory.

The third and final stage lasted from December 1948 until October 1949. The battles required great effort on both sides, but it was the Communists who enjoyed tremendous success.

THE BATTLE OF HUAI-HAI, NOVEMBER 1948–JANUARY 1949

The most decisive campaign fought in the Civil War was the Huai-Hai campaign; this brought about the start of the final stage of the conflict. Chiang had already lost control of northern China and he was determined to prevent communism spreading to the rest of China. He chose to make a stand at Xuzhou, a key site on the Longhai railway that linked central China to the GMD's capital Nanjing and to the great port of Shanghai. However, the campaign was a disaster for Chiang. The strength of the PLA was strengthened by men who had abandoned Chiang's NRA while the NRA lacked aircraft to protect its forces. In addition, as a result of Mao's order to the PLA to destroy the area surrounding Xuzhou, the Nationalists did not have enough food to feed the NRA troops. The battle lasted for more than 2 months. Chiang refused to allow the leaders of his army units to retreat, which resulted in the loss of 200,000 men. They finally surrendered on 10 January 1949.

The campaign was essential to bringing about a communist victory in the Civil War. It broke the strength of the NRA and opened up central China to the Communists. Furthermore, from that point onwards the USA was not prepared to give any more funding to the GMD. It had already given more than US$3 billion, and believed that Chiang had wasted it. Without American aid, Chiang had little chance of defeating the Communists.

By January 1949, the Communists had taken control of large areas of the north, including the capital city of Beijing. From there they moved south. By late September 1949, most of China was under communist rule. On 1 October 1949, in Tiananmen Square in Beijing, Mao declared the new government, the People's Republic of China (PRC), with himself as its leader. Chiang fled to Taiwan and set up an alternative GMD government there.

▶ **Figure 2.4** Map showing the extension of communist control in the Civil War, 1946–49

Area controlled 1946
Area controlled 1949
Additional area controlled 1950

2.4 THE REASONS FOR THE SUCCESS OF MAO AND THE CCP IN THE CIVIL WAR

LEARNING OBJECTIVES

■ Understand the military strengths and weaknesses of the Communists and the GMD

■ Understand the political strengths and weaknesses of the Communists and the GMD

■ Understand the social and economic strengths and weaknesses of the Communists and the GMD.

A victory for the Communists would not have been predicted in 1945 when the war with Japan ended. Although the GMD's performance in the Sino–Japanese War was not at all impressive, it was better equipped and held a larger proportion of territory than the Communists. Furthermore, its army was considerably larger than the PLA. However, a combination of factors resulted in the communist victory in 1949, as follows.

MILITARY REASONS

The Communists proved to be a much more effective military force than the GMD, as the following table shows.

	▼ COMMUNIST MILITARY STRENGTHS	▼ GMD MILITARY WEAKNESSES
Military leadership	Mao was a skilled leader who gave the overall plan for the war and allowed his generals to provide the detailed strategy. Lin Biao was an outstanding military general for the PLA. He was particularly skilled in directing guerrilla warfare.	Chiang was a poor military leader who could not give authority to those with the necessary military skills.
Military tactics	The PLA used a wide range of tactics which were adapted to the situation facing them. It used guerrilla warfare in the mountainous regions of China. Once the GMD had been weakened, the PLA was able to use conventional warfare in attacking the GMD in pitched battles in the cities.	The GMD made tactical errors, such as sending troops into Manchuria before they controlled the rest of north-eastern China. Manchuria proved to be a death trap for the GMD because it could not supply its troops. The GMD lost half a million men there.
Quality of the troops	The PLA was a disciplined army that was motivated by its belief in communism. When it passed through villages, it treated the local population with respect. This developed support for communism and encouraged men to join the Reds and villagers to give supplies to the army.	The NRA was a conscript army that was poorly supplied and cruelly treated. Poor treatment led to a high number of deaths and desertions, which reduced the strength of the army.

The differences between the CCP and GMD forces can explain the communist success to some extent. By 1949, the GMD forces were so weak that, with no hope of victory, Chiang was forced to retreat to Taiwan while the Communists claimed control of China.

SOURCE G

Volunteers from the Communist Chinese Army constructing a road. The People's Liberation Army was disciplined to treat civilians with respect and honesty, contrasting with Nationalists troops' thieving and abuse.

POLITICAL REASONS

It was not only the military strengths that secured victory for the CCP; the political success of communism attracted significant support for Mao's cause and encouraged much support for the CCP in the Chinese population. This meant that the CCP was more likely to receive assistance from local populations during the Civil War.

The strength of the CCP came firstly from its political unity. Mao's leadership was unchallenged, and this created a secure **chain of command** that prevented disputes during the Civil War. Furthermore, the involvement of local populations in committees to discuss reforms in the areas under communist control created a positive impression of what might be called a 'democratic dictatorship', in which government would be seen as acting for the benefit of the masses. This image was strengthened by the skilful use of propaganda. The CCP used posters as a means of spreading key messages, as well as relying on the PLA troops, who were **indoctrinated** with communist ideals, to win over local populations by treating peasants kindly.

By contrast, during the Sino–Japanese War and even more so during the Civil War, the political position of the GMD was weakening. The GMD government was corrupt and unskilled. Chiang had come to power promising to implement Sun Yat-sen's 'Three Principles of the People', but this had not happened. Chiang had set up a dictatorship rather than a democracy, and had favoured the bankers, merchant and landlords rather than the mass of the population in the countryside. His local officials had abused their power and taken bribes. This meant that the GMD was never able to raise enough taxes to fund the government and introduce effective reforms. There was little political support left for the GMD by October 1949.

KEY TERM

indoctrinate instructing someone in an ideology in such a way that they will only accept that point of view

ECONOMIC AND SOCIAL REASONS

The economic and social strength of the CCP lay in its support from the peasants, the great mass of the population of China. Mao had been correct in seeing that Chinese communism could not be achieved by a concentration on the working class alone, as Stalin, the leader of the Soviet Union, had advised him. A crucial element in securing the support of the peasants was the introduction of land reform in the countryside. During the Civil War, the CCP introduced land reforms that took away land from the richer peasantry and gave it to the poorer villagers. This often involved poorer peasants criticising their richer neighbours and frequently involved the use of violence. Furthermore, those peasants who took part in such actions had much to fear from a return of the GMD. They were committed to supporting the CCP because they risked the revenge of the landlords if the GMD took back the village.

The support of the middle classes was also important to the communist victory. They were important in the towns and cities. Many teachers, students and policemen were won over to the CCP as a result of its loyalty to China that it had demonstrated when it resisted the Japanese, which differed from the initial GMD policy of allowing the Japanese to take land.

The economic and social record of the GMD was poor. Chiang had printed money in order to finance his government. This had devalued the currency and led to high inflation, which destroyed the savings of the middle class, on whom he relied for support. Chiang introduced reforms to repair this damage, including reissuing the currency, so that the old currency, in which people had lost confidence, was withdrawn. He also introduced wage controls and new taxes. However, it was too little, too late and Chiang lost the support of the middle classes. This left him without a support base, because he had never seen the need to win over the peasants.

ACTIVITY

1 How did the leadership of China change in the years 1900–49?
2 Work with a partner to draw a timeline of all the changes in China's leadership during these years. You will need to look back at Chapter 1 to complete this task.

EXTEND YOUR KNOWLEDGE

The bad management of the economy by the GMD led to violence in GMD-controlled areas. Some workers did not go to work because the currency had almost no value. They therefore turned to robbery. Other workers went on strike and organised rebellions. To restore control, the GMD made lists of suspects and murdered those on their list. As a result, many people regarded the Communists as a better alternative government.

SOURCE H

Crowds in Beijing, China, welcome victorious communist troops following the withdrawal of Nationalist forces from the city, 31 January 1949. A portrait of Mao Zedong is being carried in the centre.

EXAM-STYLE QUESTION

A01   **A02**

SKILLS ▶ ADAPTIVE LEARNING

Explain **two** causes of the communist victory in the Civil War.   **(8 marks)**

HINT

This question is about causation. When explaining the reasons why something happened, you should identify two reasons and write a detailed paragraph for each reason to explain how it led to the outcome. Better answers will demonstrate that reasons are linked to one another.

RECAP

RECALL QUESTIONS

1 How many Communists set off on the Long March, and how many survived?
2 What tactic did Mao Zedong use to escape from the GMD on the Long March?
3 Suggest three reasons why the Long March was a significant event in Chinese history.
4 What was Chiang's initial response to the Japanese invasion of China?
5 Describe the events that led to the establishment of a second United Front.
6 Why was the bombing of Pearl Harbor in December 1941 an important event in the Sino–Japanese War?
7 Which areas of China were controlled by the GMD, and which areas were held by the CCP at the end of the war in 1945?
8 Why was the GMD defeated in the Battle of Huai-Hai?
9 What methods of propaganda were used by the CCP to attract support during the Civil War?
10 Why was the GMD unpopular with the peasants?

CHECKPOINT

STRENGTHEN

S1 Write a paragraph describing the events of the Long March.
S2 What help did America give to the GMD during the Sino–Japanese War and the Civil War?
S3 List three reasons why the CCP won the Civil War.

CHALLENGE

C1 Write the reasons for the Long March on cards, putting one reason on each card. Organise them into a list, with the most important at the top and the least important at the bottom. Compare your list with a partner. Have you placed the cards in the same order? Discuss any differences.
C2 Compare the political and social influence of the GMD and the CCP during the Civil War. Draw up a table with two columns: one for the GMD and one for the CCP, and two rows headed political and social. List their influences. Highlight the points that are similar.
C3 In what ways did the external influences on China change in the years 1934–49? Draw a large concept map with one leg for each country that was involved in Chinese affairs during this period. Develop it by noting down their actions and influence. Use it to help you write two or three short paragraphs describing the changes.

SUMMARY

- The encirclement of the Jiangxi Soviet by the GMD in October 1934 forced the Communists to break out and begin the Long March north in search of a safe base.
- Mao Zedong emerged as the undisputed leader of the CCP during the Long March.
- After a year in which the Communists were under constant attack by the GMD and had to endure extremely difficult conditions, they reached the safety of Yanan and established a base there.
- In 1937, Chiang established a second United Front with the Communists in order to fight against the Japanese, who had invaded and were expanding control of China.
- The Communist's Red Army grew in popularity during the Sino–Japanese War. In contrast, the GMD lost support because of its violent treatment of peasants and soldiers.
- Chiang had always regarded the CCP as the main enemy, and in 1946 civil war broke out between the CCP and the GMD for control of China.
- The Communists' military, political and social advantages allowed them to defeat the GMD in the Civil War.
- On 1 October 1949, Mao declared the establishment of the People's Republic of China.

EXAM GUIDANCE: PART (B) QUESTIONS

A01   **A02**

SKILLS   ADAPTIVE LEARNING

Question to be answered: Explain two causes of the survival of Communists on the Long March 1934–35.   (8 marks)

1   **Analysis Question 1: What is the question type testing?**
In this question, you have to demonstrate that you have knowledge and understanding of the key features and characteristics of the period studied. In this particular case, it is knowledge and understanding of the Long March 1934–35.

You also have to explain, analyse and make judgements about historical events and periods to explain why something happened.

2   **Analysis Question 2: What do I have to do to answer the question well?**
Obviously you have to write about the Long March! However, this is not just a case of writing everything you know. You have to write about why Communists survived. To do this well, you need to give the detail showing what caused the survival to happen, but you need to make sure you are explaining why that detail actually led to their survival. We call this explaining why your chosen causes produced the given outcome (in this case, the survival of Communists).

So in this case, there are many causes of the survival of Communists on the Long March. You might write about the impact of Mao's role and the tactics he used, for example.

3   **Analysis Question 3: Are there any techniques I can use to make it very clear that I am doing what is needed to be successful?**
This is an 8-mark question and you need to make sure you leave enough time to answer the other two questions fully (they are worth 22 marks in total). Therefore, you need to get straight in to writing your answer. The question asks for two causes, so it is a good idea to write two paragraphs and to begin each paragraph with phrases like 'One cause was…' and 'Another cause was...'. You will get a maximum of 4 marks for each cause that you explain, so make sure you include two causes.

How many marks you score for each cause will depend on how well you use accurate and factual information to explain why the Communists survived.

Answer A

There were two reasons why Communists survived the Long March. Mao was a great leader and the Communists treated the peasants well when they passed through their villages.

What are the strengths and weaknesses of Answer A?
It is not a very good answer. It has the strength of setting out two reasons, but it has not given factual information to support those reasons, or explained why these reasons caused the survival of Communists. It is doubtful that this answer would score more than two marks.

Answer B

There were two reasons why Communists survived the Long March.

The first reason was that Mao was a great leader and his tactics helped Communists to survive. Mao took control of the CCP after the meeting at Zunyi in January 1935. He developed a tactic of constantly changing directions and dividing the Red Army and then grouping together again. This tactic made it really difficult for the GMD to pursue the Communists and so that helped them to survive. The clever leadership of Mao inspired the Communists into great acts of bravery like crossing the Dadu River on a chain bridge and this meant that at the end of the march 10,000 had survived.

Another reason why Communists survived the Long March was because they treated the peasants well. When they entered a village they did not attack the peasants and they made sure that they were polite and did not steal their property. They taught the villagers about communism, so the villagers were more likely to support the Communists and not help the GMD to hunt down the Communists. This helped Communists to survive and get to Yanan.

What are the strengths and weaknesses of Answer B?
This is an excellent answer. It gives two causes and provides factual support in showing how those causes brought about their survival. It would be likely to receive full marks.

Challenge a friend
Use the Student Book to set a part (b) question for a friend. Then look at the answer. Does it do the following things?

☐ Provide two causes
☐ Provide detailed information to support the causes
☐ Show how the causes led to the given outcome.

If it does, you can tell your friend that the answer is very good!

3. CHANGE UNDER MAO, 1949–63

世界人民大[　]团[　]

LEARNING OBJECTIVES

■ Understand the impact of the changes Mao introduced in agriculture and industry

■ Understand changes to the lives of women and the extent of their success

■ Understand Mao's political changes including Thought Reform and the Hundred Flowers Campaign and the influence of the Soviet Union on China.

In the years 1949–63, China experienced a rapid and far-reaching period of change as Chairman Mao, leader of the Chinese Communist Party (CCP), tried to establish a communist system and society. The lives of peasants were transformed by the establishment of collectives. Attempts were made to achieve rapid industrialisation to allow China to modernise its economy. There were also significant changes in the lives of women as the Communists tried to end the inequalities. Perhaps the greatest changes were the political changes. Mao tried to establish a Chinese communist system, which required changing the way that people thought as well as changing the way China was ruled by its political system. Finally, Mao attempted to establish China's role in the wider world by developing a relationship with the only communist superpower, the Soviet Union. The relationship with the Soviet Union was one of suspicion, but it did play an important role in helping China to modernise during the 1950s.

3.1 CHANGES IN AGRICULTURE

LEARNING OBJECTIVES

- Understand the attack on the landlords and the Agrarian Reform Law 1950
- Understand the reasons for the collectivisation of agriculture
- Understand the stages leading to collectivisation and its consequences.

When Mao became the leader of China in 1949, he had a very clear idea of what he wanted to achieve:

- the establishment of a communist system, in the way that it was ruled, the way the economy was run and in the way people lived their lives
- the modernisation of China's economy.

The first step towards communism would be in the countryside. Modernisation required the movement of the population from the country to the town and sufficient food to feed urban workers. This is because a modern economy is based on industrial production. Mao needed more workers in the towns to develop modern industry, but he also needed to be certain that there would be enough food produced on the farms to feed everyone in the towns and countryside. Mao believed that this could be achieved by reforming agriculture into a communist system of production.

KEY TERM

collectivisation the organisation of agricultural land into one great area of land which was farmed communally by the peasants rather than them working on small individual farms

THE ATTACK ON THE LANDLORDS AND THE AGRARIAN REFORM LAW 1950

During the years of struggle, Mao had correctly identified that the achievement of a communist system depended on the support of the peasants, who made up most of the population of China. In the soviet at Yanan, before the war, and in the areas that the Communists had occupied during the war, Mao had ordered that the peasants be treated with respect. In particular he stressed that richer peasants were to be treated with moderation and that attacks should be targeted on larger landlords who bullied the peasants. After the victory in the Civil War, Mao continued to argue for this type of modest reform. He did not want to make the mistakes made in the Soviet Union during the 1930s, when the **collectivisation** of agriculture had led to peasant resistance and millions had starved to death.

EXTEND YOUR KNOWLEDGE

Stalin's policy of collectivisation in the Soviet Union was not supported by many of the peasants. His attempt to force them to give to the state all their property and to join the collectives was resisted by the peasants, who destroyed their animals and grain. Stalin called these peasants kulaks and imprisoned them in their region with no food. This action led to a great man-made famine in the years 1932–33, in which between 10 and 15 million peasants died.

SOURCE A

From Chairman Mao's directive issued to CCP members in 1948.

Land reform should be divided into two stages. In the first stage strike blows at the landlords and neutralise the rich peasants. The second stage is the equal distribution of land, including the land rented out by the rich peasants and their surplus land. However, the treatment of rich peasants should differ from that of the landlords.

Reactionaries must be suppressed, but killing without discrimination is strictly forbidden; the fewer killings the better.

KEY TERM

reactionaries people who oppose new ideas and believe in returning a political system to its previous state

This view was reflected in the Agrarian Reform Law passed in 1950.

■ The property of large landlords was taken away from them and given to the peasants.

■ The property of enemies of the state, for example, Chiang Kai-shek and foreign nationals, was confiscated.

Although officially this was a moderate policy, putting the reform into action was left in the hands of the local communities. As a result, many took the opportunity to settle old disputes. Villages held 'struggle meetings' where they denounced rich landlords and violence followed. It is estimated that up to a million landlords were executed, thousands were beaten up and thousands more sent to special camps, where they were 're-educated' to accept communist ideas. Thus, the Agrarian Reform Law brought about the destruction of the old **elite** and won over to communism vast numbers of peasants who benefited from the removal of the landlords.

KEY TERM

elite people of the highest and usually wealthiest class

SOURCE B

A photograph taken in 1952, showing Huang Chin-Chi, a farmer from the province of Kwantung, before a people's tribunal. He owned just two-thirds of an acre of land, but was still found guilty of exploitation and shot.

ACTIVITY

1 Refresh your memory of the main ideas of communism and study Source A. In what ways does this show how the Agrarian Reform Law brought about changes in China?

2 Make a list of the consequences of the Agrarian Reform Law.

THE COLLECTIVISATION OF AGRICULTURE

■ Once the landlord class had been removed, the peasants were encouraged to share their equipment, animals and work in **mutual aid teams** consisting of ten or fewer households, to farm the land. However, the land was still owned individually by the peasants. By the end of 1952, about 40 per cent of peasants belonged to mutual aid teams.

■ The next stage of the progress towards achieving communism in the countryside was the establishment of Agricultural Producers Co-operatives (APCs). The land was still owned by the peasants but needed to be managed centrally because an APC was a large unit that included the animals, equipment and labour of 3–5 mutual aid teams (30–50 households). The formation of APCs was encouraged by Mao from 1953, because he believed it would be the most effective way of increasing production of food. The APCs also created a demand for machinery, which boosted industry as well as allowing much greater production of food in the countryside.

■ The creation of APCs was most successful in areas where mutual aid teams already existed. However, in some areas, richer peasants took the opportunity to buy up large sections of the land and hired labour to work on it. This recovery of capitalism undermined the purpose of the APCs and led to interference by communist officials, who began to force peasants into APCs. The result was peasant resistance similar to that in the Soviet Union in the 1930s. Richer peasants killed their animals and burned their crops rather than hand them over to the APC. In January 1955, Mao called for a temporary halt to the APCs. However, by the summer he decided that the party needed to push ahead with APCs and move to the next stage with the introduction of **collectives** or **communes**.

■ The process of collectivisation of agriculture intensified in 1956 and especially from 1958, when Mao introduced the Great Leap Forward (see page 49). Collectives were farms made up of 2,000–3,000 households. All the land, animals and equipment belonged to the collective and there was no **private** ownership. One reason why Mao was so anxious to push forward with the programme was because he believed that the peasants were harming his effort to industrialise China by overeating instead of sending their extra food to the towns. In the collectives, the produce would not be the property of the peasants and the party would be able to direct it to the towns. By the end of 1958, about 700 million people had been placed in the collective farms. These farms were run by more than 26,000 communes that were established across China.

KEY TERM

commune organised regions where all the collectives were grouped together

---

SOURCE C

A poster showing Mao Zedong with the farmers from Guangdong, at the time of the foundation of the popular communes.

Stage 4
Collectivisation
1958–62

Stage 3
Agricultural
Producers
Co-operatives
1953–56

Stage 2
Mutual Aid Teams
1951–55

Stage 1
Agrarian Reform
Law and the attack
on landlords 1950

▲ **Figure 3.1** Stages in land reform, 1950–62

ACTIVITY

Read this short extract from a speech made by Chairman Mao in 1955 to an audience of communist officials and peasants, explaining why it is necessary to introduce collectivisation.

A new socialist mass movement can be created in the Chinese countryside. But some of our comrades are tottering along like a woman with bound feet, always complaining that others are going too fast. They imagine that by grumbling unnecessarily and putting up numerous barriers, they will guide the socialist mass movement in the rural areas in the right direction.

No! This is not the right way at all. It is wrong!

Finish writing this speech, explaining why it is necessary to introduce collectivisation. Remember to be as convincing as you can.

THE GREAT FAMINE, 1958–62

The result of forced collectivisation was a disaster. Mao claimed that collectivisation was wanted by the peasants, but this was merely propaganda. Collectivisation was forced on the peasants and they reacted by reducing production. At the same time, Mao also interfered with traditional farming methods. The result was a huge decline in production and consequently a wide-scale famine.

A number of factors contributed to the Great Famine:

- **No incentives** – the peasants no longer had any reason to produce more food than would meet their immediate needs, because they could not sell extra produce for a profit.
- **The Four Noes Campaign (also known as the Four Pests Campaign)** – Mao launched a campaign to get rid of sparrows, flies, mosquitoes and rats because they were pests that ate the crops and grain. Peasants were encouraged to make as much noise as possible to drive sparrows and other wild birds off the land. However, without any birds, the insects and caterpillars multiplied and ate even more crops and grain.
- **Political pressures** – Mao believed the poor scientific claims of Soviet scientists who said they had developed methods that would increase the crop by up to 16 times more than by using traditional methods. They were wrong, but peasants who tried to use traditional farming methods were denounced by communist officials as enemies of the state.
- **Fear** – communist officials did not dare speak out about the failure of production, and in order to impress Mao they lied about production.
- **Natural causes** – there was a drought in the north which reduced the harvest and flooding in the south which damaged the crops.

The famine caused 50 million deaths in China. Parents sold their children and husbands sold their wives in order to buy food. Some even resorted to cannibalism. The worst hit area was Tibet, where over 1 million people died: a quarter of the population. The people of Tibet had resisted the drive for communism and as punishment, the CCP deliberately chose to extend famine to the region. They forced the Tibetan peasants to abandon their traditional crop of barley and keeping yaks, and forced them to grow wheat and corn. The soil was not suitable for these crops, and so production failed and starvation resulted.

EXTEND YOUR KNOWLEDGE

The Communist Party did everything it could to prevent Mao from knowing about the failure in production. They lifted the crops from the fields and placed them next to the railways tracks so that when Mao travelled though China, he would see fields full of crops. When his train had passed by, they would dig up the crops and return them to their original fields.

EXTEND YOUR KNOWLEDGE

Trofim Lysenk, a Soviet scientist, claimed his method of growing 'super crops' would make weeds change into crops. This theory of 'Lysenkoism' was wrong and China suffered by using bad science.

EXTRACT A

From Jung Chang's account of the Great Famine in her book, *Wild Swans*, published in 1991. Juang Chang was born in China in 1952 and lived through the momentous events that transformed China into a communist state.

Years later I met an old colleague of my father's, a very kind and capable man, not given to exaggeration. He told me with great emotion what he had seen during the famine in one particular commune … One day a peasant burst into his room and threw himself on the floor, screaming that he had committed a terrible crime and begging to be punished. Eventually it came out that he had killed his own baby and eaten it. Hunger had been like an uncontrollable force driving him to take up the knife. With tears rolling down his cheeks, the official ordered the peasant to be arrested. Later [the peasant] was shot as a warning to baby killers.

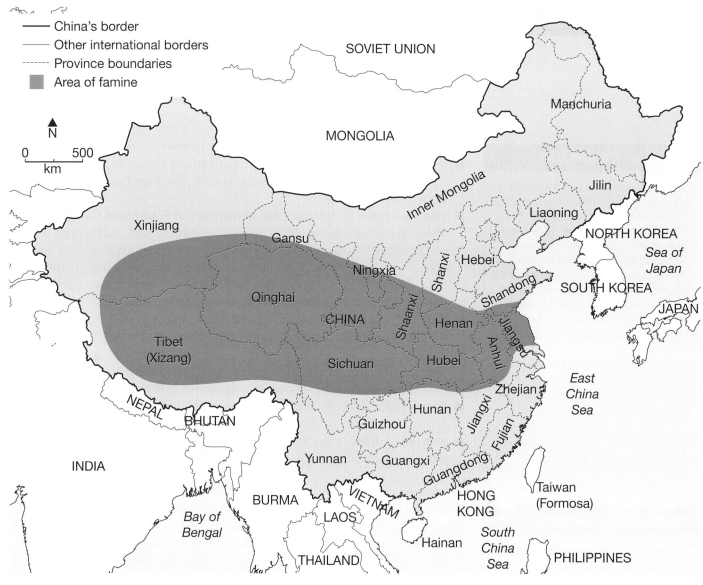

Legend:
- — China's border
- — Other international borders
- ---- Province boundaries
- ▨ Area of famine

▲ **Figure 3.2** A map showing the worst affected areas in the Great Famine, 1958–62

EXAM-STYLE QUESTION

A01 **A02**

SKILLS ▶ ADAPTIVE LEARNING

Explain **two** causes of the Great Famine, 1958–62. **(8 marks)**

HINT

This question is about causation. When explaining the reasons why something happened, you should identify two reasons and write a paragraph for each reason giving some precise details to explain how it led to the outcome.

3.2 CHANGES IN INDUSTRY

LEARNING OBJECTIVES

■ Understand the first Five Year Plan 1952–57

■ Understand the reasons for the Great Leap Forward

■ Understand the effects of the Great Leap Forward.

THE FIRST FIVE YEAR PLAN, 1952–57

Mao wanted to develop China's industry and modernise the country. The Soviet Union had demonstrated that this could be achieved through a communist system and central planning. Hundreds of Soviet advisers and specialists were welcomed into China to provide the knowledge and expertise needed for Mao to launch his industrialisation programme. By 1952, the land reforms had begun to push up agricultural output and to provide food for an urban workforce, and so Mao felt confident that he could follow his plans for industry. In December he announced the first Five Year Plan, with a focus on the rapid expansion of heavy industry, coal, iron and steel and **petroleum**. Ambitious targets were set to expand industry. The plan was put into operation at the start of 1953 and ran until 1957. It was very successful. The urban population were willing to work hard to achieve the goals and China was a land rich with natural resources that could be exploited. Some amazing achievements of construction occurred including the building of a road and rail bridge across the Yangzi River at Nanjing.

Although we have to be cautious about the results, since the officials were strongly motivated to overestimate the production figures, the achievements of the First Five Year Plan were impressive:

■ Coal production doubled.

■ Electric power production increased by three times the previous level.

■ Steel production increased by four times the previous level.

It was claimed that the rapid improvement in industrial production showed that the communist system was better than the capitalist system it had replaced. Central planning had been accompanied by the gradual removal of private businesses as businessmen were brought into partnership with the state or taken over completely. The results were certainly impressive enough for Mao to feel confident that China could begin a new, more ambitious programme, with the announcement of the second Five Year Plan in 1958.

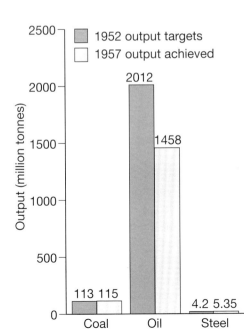

◀ **Figure 3.3** A bar chart showing the production targets and achievements of the first Five Year Plan

THE GREAT LEAP FORWARD, 1958–62

KEY TERM

Party Congress the formal meeting of the Chinese Communist Party. It meets about once every 5 years

▶ **Figure 3.4** Reasons for the Great Leap Forward

REASONS FOR THE GREAT LEAP FORWARD

The second Five Year Plan is more often known as the Great Leap Forward. It was announced, with great excitement, to the Eighth **Party Congress** in May 1958 by Liu Shaoqi. Liu called upon the people to create a new China overnight. Mao was enthusiastic about the plan and immediately announced that China would overtake Britain as an industrial power in less than 15 years. There were a number of reasons that led to the launch of the Great Leap Forward, as shown in Figure 3.4.

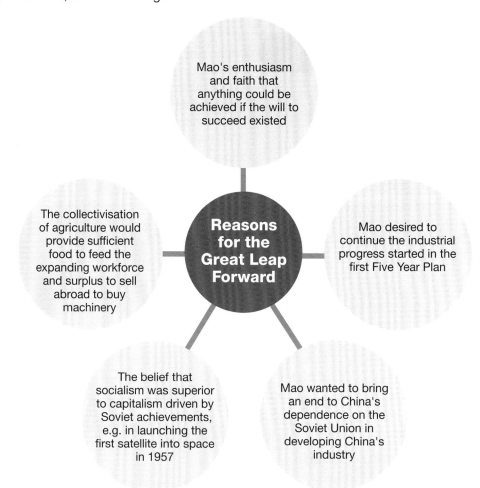

- Mao believed that anything could be achieved by the People's Republic of China (PRC) if it just had the will to succeed.
- He was convinced that communism was better than capitalism and that this had been proved by the Soviet Union's success in being the first country to launch a satellite into space.
- He believed that the policy of collectivisation would produce sufficient food to feed the expanding industrial workforce and have enough left over to sell abroad and buy machinery.
- Mao also wanted to reduce China's dependence on the Soviet Union, and he believed the Great Leap Forward would provide the rapid industrialisation that would make this possible.

Mao had come to power with the support of the peasants, but he believed that real progress would come through industrialisation. He was convinced that China could 'leap' from a rural economy to an industrial one without the disadvantages that affected a capitalist country as it moved towards a modern economy. The Great Leap Forward would happen under the slogan of 'walking on two legs'. Mao believed that China would be able to increase its agricultural production and industrial production at the same time. Soon China would be able to end its dependence on the Soviet Union, which had provided experts and loans at very high rates of interest to fund the first Five Year Plan. Mao believed that China would soon be able to use her own experts.

Key features of the Great Leap Forward included the following.
- The involvement of the whole population to achieve the targets. One way in which the enthusiasm of the workers was demonstrated was by the decision to use the manual labour of workers who dug out the soil by hand instead of using mechanical diggers.
- The collectivisation of agriculture – the change from APCs to collectives was an essential ingredient in increasing the supply of food for the urban workers (see pages 43–44).
- Backyard furnaces – the whole of China was involved in the campaign to produce steel. As many as 600,000 furnaces were set up in backyards in the towns and villages, and families melted down their metal implements. On the collective farms, men left the fields to work at the furnaces. They even melted down their farming tools and equipment.
- Privately owning businesses came to an end and all businesses were taken over by the state. This allowed the CCP to control exactly what was produced by industry and to achieve another step towards a communist system by removing private property and profits.
- Massive projects – giant bridges, canals and dams were constructed. The Chinese newspapers praised the economic achievements of communism.

ACTIVITY

Work in our group to write and perform a 'radio broadcast' that gives the arguments in favour of the Great Leap Forward. The broadcast should last 30 seconds.

SOURCE E

A backyard furnace used during the Great Leap Forward.

THE EFFECTS OF THE GREAT LEAP FORWARD

SOURCE F

From Mao's speech to Party Leaders in 1959.

Coal and iron cannot walk by themselves. They need vehicles to transport them. This I did not foresee. I and the Premier did not concern ourselves with this point. You could say we were ignorant of it. I am a complete outsider when it comes to economic construction. I understand nothing about industrial planning. The main responsibility was mine and you should take me to task. The chaos created was on a grand scale, and I must take responsibility. But, Comrades, you must all analyse your own responsibility.

It cannot be denied the Great Leap Forward produced some outstanding achievements of labour. In 1958, 11 million tonnes of steel were produced, and there were huge rises in the production of coal, wood, cement and fertiliser in that year. However, overall the Great Leap Forward was a terrible failure.

- Collectivisation failed and 50 million died in the famine.
- The steel produced in the backyard furnaces was of poor quality and had to be thrown away by the officials who collected it. Only steel produced in the large factories could be used in industrial production.
- Production in businesses decreased, as without the profit motive there was no reason to work hard.
- The Soviet experts left China in 1960, but the Chinese were not yet sufficiently trained to manage without them (see page 79).

As early as 1959, even Mao admitted that the Great Leap Forward had failed, when he commented on his own limitations as an economic planner and instructed party members to reflect on their own failings. The Great Leap Forward seriously damaged Mao politically. He resigned as head of state and for the next few years was rarely seen in public.

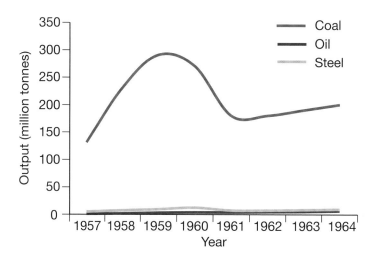

▶ **Figure 3.5** A graph showing the failures of the Great Leap Forward

ACTIVITY

Create a large mind map summarising the aims, policies, achievements and failures of Mao's policies to modernise China's industry. Try to add at least three points to each branch. Colour-code the branches to make them easier to remember.

EXAM-STYLE QUESTION

A01 **A02**

Explain **two** ways in which Chinese agriculture in 1960 was different from Chinese agriculture in 1949. **(6 marks)**

HINT

The question is about comparison. So make sure you explain how things are different, and don't just give the information about agriculture in the two periods.

3.3 CHANGES IN THE ROLE OF WOMEN

LEARNING OBJECTIVES

■ Understand communist attitudes to women

■ Understand the Marriage Law of 1950

■ Understand the changes in the lives of women 1950–62.

To achieve a communist society, Mao needed to end unequal treatment of women. For centuries, Chinese culture had treated women as second-class citizens. They were the properties first of their fathers, then of their husbands, and widows were even under the control of their eldest sons. The birth of a son was celebrated, but a daughter was regarded as a costly expense. Girls received little, if any, education and many were pushed by their fathers into an arranged marriage when they were teenagers. Potential husbands expected to be paid a **dowry** once the marriage had happened. Furthermore, women could not own property, the **constitution** did not allow them to vote, and while their husbands could divorce them, wives did not have the right to divorce their husbands. Rich and powerful men often kept women as **concubines**.

Mao had shown his commitment to equal rights for women in the Jiangxi and Yanan soviets. The CCP had insisted that women were the equals of men and it made certain practices illegal, such as foot-binding. It was not surprising, therefore, that one of the earliest acts of the CCP was to pass a Marriage Law in 1950.

EXTEND YOUR KNOWLEDGE

Mao was particularly opposed to arranged marriages, having refused to agree to his own arranged marriage to his older cousin Luo Yigu when he was 14 years old – even though the bride's family had paid the dowry. He refused to live with Luo. In 1919, he wrote a series of newspaper articles criticising the practice of arranged marriage and the way that wives seemed to be the slaves of their husbands.

The 1950 Marriage Law stated that:
■ arranged marriage and the payment of a dowry was banned
■ the minimum age of marriage was raised to 18 years for women and 20 years for men
■ keeping concubines was forbidden
■ both men and women had equal rights to request a divorce
■ men and women in arranged marriages were entitled to divorce their partner
■ women were given property rights to own, buy and sell property
■ **infanticide** was forbidden.

KEY TERM

infanticide the practice of killing young babies, usually by their parents. Baby girls were particularly at risk

EXTEND YOUR KNOWLEDGE

Male children were valued much more than girls in China. Many Chinese believed that without a son, there would be no descendants, because only males could pass on the family name. Girls were expensive to raise, and when they married, a dowry had to be paid to their husband's family. Once married, they cared for their husband's parents and not their own. Therefore, it was not unusual for a baby girl to be killed shortly after birth. This practice continued after the introduction of communism, and it increased after the introduction of the one-child policy in 1979.

The CCP also introduced policies to transform the role of women in the family. It was traditional for families to be large, especially in rural areas. This increased the risk of women dying in childbirth. In 1953, the CCP:

■ introduced policies promoting birth control
■ began training midwives to adopt procedures that made childbirth safer.

Furthermore, collectivisation promised to reduce the many tasks for women who were managing the home by providing mess halls for communal eating. This allowed women to play a greater role in the economic life of the country.

Changes for women extended further than marriage and family; the CCP was also eager to get women involved in the political life of the country. In the Electoral Law of 1953, women were given equal voting rights. The All China Women's Federation, established in 1949 to promote policies towards women, sent officials into rural areas to encourage women to participate in politics at local levels by joining committees and party groups.

The following table summarises the impact of the policies towards women.

▼ POLICY AREA	▼ IMPACT
Marriage	■ Peasants opposed the Marriage Law, especially in the western areas where there was a large Muslim population. ■ The use of matchmakers to arrange marriages continued. ■ Rural marriages continued with the exchange of gifts. ■ Women who divorced their husbands were treated as outcasts. ■ The average age of marriage rose in the 1950s. ■ Cases of infanticide were reduced.
Family life	■ In 1954, China's biggest pharmaceutical company began producing contraceptives. ■ There was resistance to birth control in rural areas. ■ Childbirth became safer with the use of trained midwives and procedures such as sterilisation of medical equipment.
Economic role	■ Women's property rights did not last long; private property was outlawed in the campaign for collectivisation. ■ Husbands resorted to wife-selling during the famine. ■ Literacy levels among women rose. ■ The proportion of women in the workforce rose from 8 per cent in 1949 to 29 per cent by the mid-1960s.
Political role	■ In 1949, 69 women were elected to the Central People's Political Consultative Committee, accounting for just 10 per cent of its membership. ■ In the 1953 election to the National People's Congress, 12 per cent of the deputies elected were women. ■ Women's participation in politics was opposed by men but there was some acceptance that women could hold minor roles. ■ The first Minister of Health and the first Minister of Justice in the PRC were both women. ■ Between 1949 and 1962, women's participation in politics increased, with women being elected to neighbourhood committees and co-operatives.

ACTIVITY

How far did the role of women in China change from 1900 to 1962?

Draw up a table with two columns: 1900–49 and 1949–62. In the first column, list how women were treated before the Communists took control. In the second column, list how women were treated under Mao's government. Highlight all the ways in which women's lives had changed.

Remember to distinguish between what the CCP wanted – to achieve a communist society in which everyone was equal – and what actually happened.

SOURCE G

A propaganda poster from the 1950s showing the ideal communist woman, an equal member of society taking her place as a soldier in the PLA.

3.4 POLITICAL CHANGES

LEARNING OBJECTIVES

■ Understand the importance of Mao Zedong in the government of the PRC

■ Understand Thought Reform and the Antis Campaigns

■ Understand the Hundred Flowers Campaign and its consequences.

The victory of the Communists in the Civil War brought in an era of important political change in China. The new government was led by Mao Zedong who, as Chairman of the Communist Party, held the ultimate authority in government. In theory, China was a democratic country:

■ Every adult had the right to vote.

■ Elections were held across the country in the towns and villages.

■ It was claimed that power was in the hands of the people.

The reality was very different: the Communist Party was the only political party allowed and its leading members held the key positions in the new republic. Government was carried out by the Politburo, an organisation of leading members of the CCP, which was controlled by Mao. Furthermore, Mao was suspicious of any criticism and because he wielded such great power, it was unlikely that anyone with opposing ideas would be elected or given a position in government. The structure of the government of the PRC is outlined in Figure 3.6.

▶ **Figure 3.6** The structure of the government of the PRC

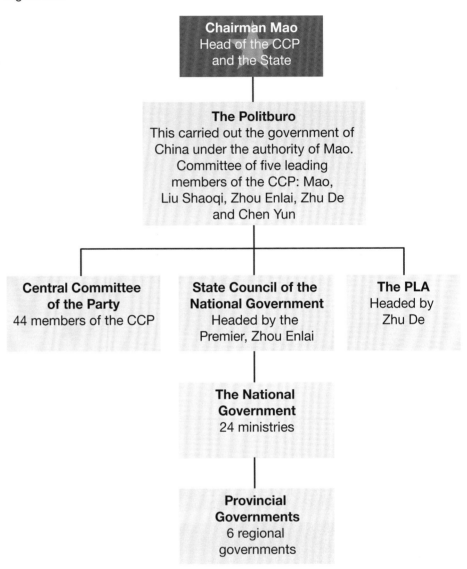

Chairman Mao
Head of the CCP and the State

The Politburo
This carried out the government of China under the authority of Mao. Committee of five leading members of the CCP: Mao, Liu Shaoqi, Zhou Enlai, Zhu De and Chen Yun

Central Committee of the Party
44 members of the CCP

State Council of the National Government
Headed by the Premier, Zhou Enlai

The PLA
Headed by Zhu De

The National Government
24 ministries

Provincial Governments
6 regional governments

KEY TERM

counter-revolutionary idea that or person who opposes a revolution and tries to reverse it. Mao was particularly worried about those who still had sympathies for the GMD

The political system and the way in which government was conducted were based upon Mao Zedong's beliefs. This was known as Mao Zedong Thought and included ideas such as class struggle and the need for continuing revolution to prevent **counter-revolutionary** ideas entering China and threatening the revolution. Mao believed in the mass organisation of the ordinary people to drive the revolution. He was determined that China would not be controlled by the Soviet Union. He promoted the slogan 'self-reliance' to show China was an independent communist country.

▶ **Figure 3.7** A summary of Mao Zedong Thought

THOUGHT REFORM AND THE ANTIS CAMPAIGNS

By 1951, the structure of the government was in place, GMD supporters had been rounded up and sent to re-education camps, and the people had been brought under control by requiring them to be registered in a region and obliging them to obtain permission to move from one area to another. However, Mao was not satisfied that the CCP had complete authority. In particular, he was deeply suspicious of **intellectuals** whose views were different to his and especially of those who had been educated abroad. Therefore, in September 1951 the CCP launched a Thought Reform Campaign that was focused on forcing intellectuals in universities to confess to the errors in their thinking and to attend study sessions to re-educate them in Mao Zedong Thought.

Mao also suspected party members of moving away from his teaching and businessmen of secretly supporting capitalist ideas. Therefore, in 1951 and 1952 he launched the Three Antis and the Five Antis Campaigns.

	▼ THE THREE ANTIS CAMPAIGN, 1951	▼ THE FIVE ANTIS CAMPAIGN, 1952
Targets	Party members and **bureaucrats**	Businessmen
Aims	To combat: 1 corruption 2 waste 3 inefficiency.	To bring an end to: 1 bribery 2 avoiding paying taxes 3 theft of state property 4 fraud 5 industrial sabotage.

The campaigns were conducted through mass meetings, where loyal citizens were encouraged to denounce officials and employers who they considered guilty of offences. Those denounced were encouraged to make public confessions and were punished by fines or sent to labour camps. The humiliation was so great that it is estimated that 2–3 million committed suicide.

The campaigns did have the effect that Mao wanted: there was a huge increase in support for the party and a reduction in the activity of criminal gangs in large cities like Shanghai.

THE HUNDRED FLOWERS CAMPAIGN, 1957

In 1957, Mao appeared to change his mind. Although, in 1955, he had ordered the punishment of the intellectual Hu Feng who had written that there should be more freedom in artistic creation, it seems that Mao was becoming more open to allowing debate. In early 1957, he announced that the people were to 'let a hundred flowers bloom'. In other words, Mao was encouraging free speech and he called on intellectuals and artists to say where the party and government had gone wrong in their efforts to create a communist state. Historians have suggested a number of reasons why Mao made this announcement.

■ China needed the educated classes for its industrial development and the lack of intellectual freedom was preventing scientific advances.

■ Mao thought that the campaign would shake up the CCP and identify those in the CCP who were corrupt or not loyal.

■ The 1956 revolution in Hungary had demonstrated what happened when the people did not support their communist government.

■ Soviet President Nikita Khrushchev had criticised the Cult of Stalin in 1956; such criticisms could also be directed at the Cult of Mao in China.

EXTEND YOUR KNOWLEDGE

In October 1956, there was a nationwide revolt in Hungary against the Soviet Union's control of the country. It was the first major threat to the Soviet Union's control of Eastern Europe since the Second World War. The Soviet Union sent a large army into Hungary in November. The revolution was stopped and a new Soviet-controlled government was set up there.

At first, criticism was limited and focused on trivial matters. However, after the call was repeated by China's daily newspaper, the volume of criticism grew, and Mao was shocked to find that this criticism was not confined to CCP officials, but included him. It was time for him to end the campaign.

EXTEND YOUR KNOWLEDGE

In a secret meeting in February 1956, Khrushchev had denounced the Cult of Stalin in the Soviet Union and launched the process of de-Stalinisation in the Soviet Union. This process destroyed the image of Stalin as a perfect leader. Khrushchev's criticisms of the labour camps and use of terror could be applied to Mao's rule in China. Deng Xiaoping and Zhu De were present at the meeting, and when they returned to China, they saw an opportunity to limit Mao's dominance and to introduce a more collective leadership. Therefore, when the new constitution of the CCP was drawn up, all references to Mao Zedong Thought were removed.

SOURCE H

From an account of Mao's reaction to the criticism in the Hundred Flowers Campaign by his doctor, Zhisui Li.

Mao … was shocked. He had never intended that any of the criticisms be directed against him. He had never meant the party as an institution to come under attack. Accustomed as he was to the flattery of everyone he met, certain that his real enemies had been eliminated or put in jail, he had not realised the depth of intellectuals' dissatisfaction.

Mao had grossly miscalculated. He stayed in bed, depressed and apparently immobilized … He was rethinking his strategy, plotting his revenge. He was furious.

ACTIVITY

Working together with a partner, decide who will represent the peasants and who will represent the workers. Each make a list of the criticisms you have of Mao's government. Compare your lists. Which criticisms are the same and which are different?

SOURCE I

A propaganda poster from the early 1960s showing leading members of the CCP Zhou Enlai, Liu Shaoqi, Peng Dehuai and Mao Zedong in a perfect landscape.

KEY TERM

rightist anyone who criticised the CCP and appeared to favour capitalism and criticise collectivisation. These people held right-wing political views

ACTIVITY

Examine Source I. Explain why this might have been an effective propaganda poster.

Mao's response to the criticism was to stop the Hundred Flowers Campaign and launch instead an Anti-Rightist Campaign. Critics were now labelled as **rightists** and forced to confess their evil thoughts before being sent to re-education camps for sentences of up to 20 years. It is estimated that the victims included between half a million and three-quarters of a million party members.

The leading members of the party were not safe either. At the Lushan Conference in 1959, Peng Dehuai, the only leading party member who had criticised the famine, was denounced and replaced as Defence Minister by Lin Biao. Mao stepped down as head of state, but this move did not really affect his power, which came from his leadership of the party. In fact, it was a very clever move because he could stand aside from the failures of the party, especially regarding taking the blame for the famine.

EXAM-STYLE QUESTION

AO1 **AO2**

SKILLS ▶ ADAPTIVE LEARNING

Explain **two** causes of Mao's decision to bring an end to the Hundred Flowers Campaign.
(8 marks)

HINT

This question is about causation. When explaining the reasons why something happened, you should identify two reasons and write a paragraph for each reason giving some precise details to explain how it led to the outcome.

3.5 THE INFLUENCE OF THE SOVIET UNION ON DEVELOPMENTS IN CHINA

LEARNING OBJECTIVES

■ Understand the reasons for the Sino-Soviet relationship

■ Understand the influence of the Soviet Union on the economic development of China

■ Understand the influence of the Soviet Union on the political development of China.

TIMELINE OF SINO-SOVIET RELATIONS 1949–62

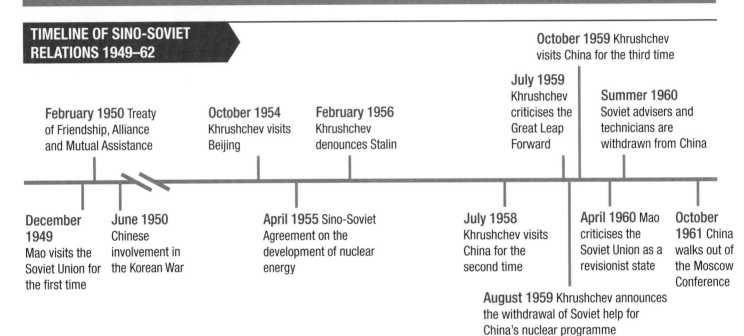

October 1959 Khrushchev visits China for the third time

July 1959 Khrushchev criticises the Great Leap Forward

Summer 1960 Soviet advisers and technicians are withdrawn from China

February 1950 Treaty of Friendship, Alliance and Mutual Assistance

October 1954 Khrushchev visits Beijing

February 1956 Khrushchev denounces Stalin

December 1949 Mao visits the Soviet Union for the first time

June 1950 Chinese involvement in the Korean War

April 1955 Sino-Soviet Agreement on the development of nuclear energy

July 1958 Khrushchev visits China for the second time

April 1960 Mao criticises the Soviet Union as a revisionist state

October 1961 China walks out of the Moscow Conference

August 1959 Khrushchev announces the withdrawal of Soviet help for China's nuclear programme

It was natural that the People's Republic of China should establish a relationship with the Soviet Union in after its victory in 1949.

■ The Soviet Union had provided military advisers to the Communists during its struggle against the GMD.

■ The Soviet Union was the leading communist country in a mainly hostile capitalist world.

However, Mao was always suspicious of Stalin and his intentions. After all, Stalin had supported the GMD originally, and even in the spring of 1949 he had suggested that the Chinese Communist Party should be happy with just controlling northern China. Nevertheless, in spite of his reservations, Mao needed to establish relations with the Soviet Union and draw on its knowledge in establishing a communist state. In particular, Mao wanted military and economic assistance from the Soviet Union and put this request to its Politburo (the main policy-making committee of the Soviet Communist Party) on his first visit to Moscow in December 1949.

A propaganda poster showing Chinese children with their two communist heroes, Mao and Stalin.

Negotiations began between the two countries and, in February 1950, a Treaty of Friendship, Alliance and Mutual Assistance was signed. The Treaty settled a number of key demands for China, including:

■ promise of aid in the event of an attack
■ a loan of US $300 million
■ a list of all Soviet agents in China.

This gave China the funding it needed to begin modernising its economy, and gave some guarantees for its safety. However, the Treaty also gave extensive economic concessions to the Soviet Union in Manchuria and Xinjiang. Mao needed to avoid focusing on these concessions, because they looked suspiciously like the unequal concessions that the Qing dynasty had granted foreigners in the late 19th and early 20th centuries, and weakened the claim that the PRC was an independent country.

SOVIET INFLUENCE ON ECONOMIC DEVELOPMENTS IN CHINA

The economic help given by the Soviet Union was of great importance to the industrialisation of China. Although the 1950 Treaty had come at a high price to China (the $300 million was a loan, not a gift), it provided 10,000 economic and military advisers, whose salaries were to be paid by the Chinese. These advisers played a vital role in establishing the first Five Year Plan. The situation improved when Nikita Khrushchev became leader of the Soviet Union. He admitted that the 1950 Treaty had been unfair to China, and in 1954, on his first visit to China, he offered a generous trade package and promised to help China develop its civilian nuclear programme. This allowed China to produce nuclear power for energy to power its industry. The Soviets did not give direct help to China to build nuclear weapons. The Soviet Union also pulled out of Manchuria.

The first Soviet nuclear scientists arrived in China in 1958. They helped the Chinese to select the Lop Nur salt lake as the site for nuclear testing and helped to build the first Chinese experimental heavy-water reactor (a nuclear reactor using unenriched uranium). Furthermore, more than 11,000 Chinese specialists and 1,000 scientists travelled to the Soviet Union, where they were trained in the new technology. Although Khrushchev had refused to help China build an atomic bomb, the training that the scientists received meant that they were then able to begin developing nuclear weapons in China. They began designing the first warhead in 1960.

The relationship between China and the Soviet Union was not an easy one. In July 1959, Khrushchev called the Great Leap Forward a foolish scheme. The following year, he announced that the Soviet Union would not be sending to China any of the nuclear hardware that had been promised. It was clear to Mao that his belief that China needed to 'walk on two legs' was correct.

KEY TERM

revisionist anyone whose set of beliefs, theories, or practices depart from the established belief – in this case, Marxist-Leninism

SOVIET INFLUENCE ON POLITICAL DEVELOPMENTS IN CHINA

EXTEND YOUR KNOWLEDGE

The Korean War began in 1950, when communist North Korea invaded capitalist South Korea. The United Nations, with the USA as its leading force, gave assistance to South Korea and, at the same time, China, with assistance from the Soviet Union, was the main force to support North Korea. The fighting continued until 1953, when an armistice was signed. No peace treaty was agreed, and so North and South Korea technically remain at war to this day.

Mao had never trusted Stalin. He blamed him for the high price that China had to pay for Soviet weapons to supply its troops in the Korean War and suspected that Stalin had encouraged China's involvement in order to weaken her and ensure that the Soviet Union remained the leading communist country. However, Mao did respect Stalin as a Communist. He was therefore extremely shocked when, in 1956, Khrushchev denounced Stalinism and criticised Stalin's cult of personality and use of terror. This carried a suggested criticism of Mao's regime in China. The reaction in the Chinese Politburo included making Mao Zedong Thought a less important part of the Constitution. It was little wonder, therefore, that the Sino-Soviet relationship began to decline from this point.

Mao was greatly angered by Khrushchev's suggestion of a joint Sino-Soviet venture in the Pacific, believing that the Soviets wanted to spy on China. Mao increasingly came to believe that Khrushchev was a **revisionist** and that China was the only true communist superpower.

SOURCE K

A photograph of Mao Zedong (centre) seeing off Soviet leader Nikita Khrushchev at Beijing airport after his official visit to the People's Republic of China in October 1959.

Relations declined further after two unsuccessful visits between the two communist leaders (see the 'Extend your knowledge' box below). In the Moscow Conference in 1958, Deng Xiaoping accused the Soviet Union of sending spies to China disguised as technical advisers and announced that the Soviet Union had betrayed the international communist movement. This increased Deng's political support and played a key role in his survival during the Cultural Revolution (see Chapter 4).

EXTEND YOUR KNOWLEDGE

Mao felt that he had been badly treated when he visited the Soviet Union, often having been left with nothing to do. He got his revenge in 1958, when he invited Khrushchev to Beijing. Khrushchev was booked into a hotel with no air conditioning and lots of mosquitos. It was tremendously uncomfortable for Khrushchev, as it was the middle of summer in Beijing. But even that was preferable to the embarrassment that followed. Mao organised talks at his private swimming pool. Mao was an excellent swimmer, but Khrushchev could not swim and had to wear a rubber ring around his waist. No progress was made in the talks, as Mao swam in the pool followed by Soviet interpreters.

EXAM-STYLE QUESTION

A01 **A02**

SKILLS PROBLEM SOLVING, REASONING, DECISION MAKING

How far did the relationship between China and the Soviet Union change in the years 1911–62?

You may use the following in your answer:
- the Bolshevik advisers sent to help the GMD after 1917
- Soviet support for the Five Year Plans 1952–62.

You **must** also use information of your own.   **(16 marks)**

HINT

This question is about changes and continuities over time. When explaining 'how far' something has changed, you need to identify what changed in the relationship and also those aspects that stayed the same. You are given two suggestions to help you consider how far the relationship changed. You will also need to make use of at least one example of your own.

RECAP

RECALL QUESTIONS

1 Why did Mao want to increase the production of food in China?
2 List two ways in which landlords were treated in the new PRC.
3 What were the three stages of development in agriculture in the years 1950–62?
4 Which was the worst hit geographical area in the Great Famine?
5 Which were the main industries targeted for expansion in the first Five Year Plan?
6 List two methods used by the CCP to increase production in the Great Leap Forward.
7 Give two ways in which the 1950 Marriage Law made Chinese women equal to men.
8 Suggest two reasons why Mao introduced the Hundred Flowers Campaign.
9 Give one consequence of the Hundred Flowers Campaign.
10 List two ways in which the Soviet Union aided the development of China's economy.

CHECKPOINT

STRENGTHEN

S1 Write a paragraph describing the changes in agriculture, 1950–62.
S2 What was the backyard furnace campaign and why did it fail?
S3 List three ways in which the Soviet Union and China worked together in the years 1949–62.

CHALLENGE

C1 Do you think that the changes introduced by Mao made women really equal to men in China?
C2 Compare the outcomes of the first Five Year Plan and the Great Leap Forward. Draw up a table with two columns: one for the first Five Year Plan and one for the Great Leap Forward. List the results for each plan. Suggest three reasons to explain the difference in the results.
C3 In what ways had China become a communist country in the years 1949–62? Draw a timeline of the years and plot the developments on it. Colour-code each development according to whether it was economic, political or social change. Use the timeline to help you write three paragraphs describing the changes.

SUMMARY

■ Mao intended to establish communism in China in the way it was ruled, in the way the economy was organised and in the way its people lived.
■ Agriculture was transformed by the removal of private ownership by landlords and by the establishment of collectives that were intended to increase the production of food to feed the growing proletariat.
■ Collectivisation led to declining production when new farming methods failed, and resulted in a famine that killed 50 million people.
■ The first Five Year Plan to modernise industry led to significant increases in the production of coal, steel and electric power.
■ The Great Leap Forward (the second Five Year Plan) was meant to achieve massive increases in production without relying on any other country.
■ The Great Leap Forward was a failure. The quality of the goods produced was poor and lack of a profit motive led to a decrease in production.
■ The Marriage Law 1950 provided equality for women and there were increased opportunities for women in the economic and political life of China.
■ Mao's teaching dominated the political development of the PRC and critics were removed in Thought Reform and the Three Antis and Five Antis campaigns.
■ The Hundred Flowers Campaign allowed greater freedom to criticise the government, but was soon ended when people began to criticise Mao.
■ The Soviet Union gave economic and political support to aid China in its development as a communist country, but by 1962 the relationship was collapsing.

EXAM GUIDANCE: PART (B) QUESTIONS

A01　**A02**

SKILLS ▶ ADAPTIVE LEARNING

Question to be answered: Explain two causes of the failure of the Great Leap Forward in the years 1958–62.
(8 marks)

1 **Analysis Question 1: What is the question type testing?**
In this question, you have to demonstrate that you have knowledge and understanding of the key features and characteristics of the period studied. In this particular case, it is knowledge and understanding of the Great Leap Forward 1958–62.

You also have to explain, analyse and make judgements about historical events and periods to explain why something happened.

2 **Analysis Question 2: What do I have to do to answer the question well?**
Obviously you have to write about the Great Leap Forward! But this is not just a case of writing everything you know. You have to write about why it failed. To do this well, you need to give the detail showing what caused the failures to happen, but you also need to make sure you explain why that detail actually led to failure. We call this explaining why your chosen causes produced the given outcome (in this case, the failure).

In this case, there are many causes of the failures of the Great Leap Forward. You might write about the impact of the backyard furnaces and the removal of incentives for workers, for example.

3 **Analysis Question 3: Are there any techniques I can use to make it very clear that I am doing what is needed to be successful?**
This is an 8-mark question and you need to make sure you leave enough time to answer the other two questions fully (they are worth 22 marks in total). Therefore, you need to get straight in to writing your answer. The question asks for two causes, so it is a good idea to write two paragraphs and to begin each paragraph with phrases like 'One cause was…' and 'Another cause was…'. You will get a maximum of 4 marks for each cause you explain, so make sure you include two causes.

How many marks you score for each cause will depend on how well you use accurate and factual information to explain why the failure occurred.

Answer A

There were two reasons why the Great Leap Forward failed. The steel made in the backyard furnaces was poor quality and the workers had no reasons to work hard.

What are the strengths and weaknesses of Answer A?

It is not a very good answer. It has the strength of setting out two reasons, but it has not given factual information to support those reasons, or explained why they caused the failure of the Great Leap Forward. It is doubtful that this answer would score more than two marks.

Answer B

There were two reasons why the Great Leap Forward failed.

The first reason was that the steel produced in the backyard furnaces was poor quality. Mao encouraged the whole population to take part in the Great Leap Forward and this led to the setting up of 600,000 furnaces in backyards in towns and villages. Families melted down all their metal, including farming tools and kitchen equipment. The problem was that the steel that they produced was of such poor quality that it could not be used in industry and so it had to be thrown away. This meant that there was not enough steel to produce the equipment that China needed and so the Great Leap Forward failed to achieve its aims.

Another reason why the Great Leap Forward failed was because there was no incentive for the people to work hard. Mao ended all private ownership of businesses. Under the communist system all enterprises were owned by the state and there were no profits. This was a problem because it meant there was no incentive for workers to work hard to earn bonuses and no profits for managers. They got paid exactly the same no matter how much they produced. This led to a slump in production in industry and the failure of the Great Leap Forward.

What are the strengths and weaknesses of Answer B?

This is an excellent answer. It gives two causes and provides factual evidence showing how those causes brought about the failure. It would be likely to receive full marks.

Challenge a friend

Use the Student Book to set a part (b) question for a friend. Then look at the answer. Does it do the following things?

☐ Provide two causes
☐ Provide detailed information to support the causes
☐ Show how the causes led to the given outcome.

If it does, you can tell your friend that the answer is very good!

4. THE CULTURAL REVOLUTION AND ITS IMPACT, 1965–76

备战备荒
为人民.

LEARNING OBJECTIVES

- Understand Mao's motives for the Cultural Revolution
- Understand the role of the Red Guards, education and the 'cult of Mao'
- Understand the impact of the Cultural Revolution on China and Mao's position.

After the disastrous events of the Great Leap Forward and the criticisms that emerged from the Hundred Flowers Campaign, Mao lost some authority in China, as the 'Rightists', led by Deng Xiaoping and Liu Shaoqi, tried to introduce less socialist policies. Although Mao was not seen regularly in public, he did not intend to give up power. His return to public life was signalled on 16 July 1966 when, at the age of 73, he swam in the Yangtze River. This very dramatic action demonstrated that he had lost none of his abilities and that he was determined to carry out the next phase of change in China. From 1966 until Mao's death 1976, life in China was turned upside down by the events of the Cultural Revolution. This new revolution attacked the old traditions that had survived the first decades of communism, in a period of great violence and upheaval in which increasingly no one in China felt safe. Leading members of the Chinese Communist Party (CCP) were removed and even members of the Red Guard found themselves among those accused of betraying communism. Only the People's Liberation Army (PLA) prevented the destruction of the system. The Cultural Revolution had an impact on the economy, society and the political system of China.

4.1 MAO'S MOTIVES FOR THE CULTURAL REVOLUTION

LEARNING OBJECTIVES

- Understand the role that party divisions played in launching the Cultural Revolution
- Understand the role that Mao's ideology played in launching the Cultural Revolution
- Understand the immediate stages in launching the Cultural Revolution.

Mao was rarely seen in public in the years after 1962. His withdrawal had allowed him to sidestep the blame for the many failures of the Great Leap Forward and the famine. However, his absence from public view did not mark his retirement from politics. From the sidelines he observed the actions of CCP leaders, including Liu Shaoqi and Deng Xiaoping, with increasing disapproval. By 1965 he was ready to return to active politics and to save the revolution from being destroyed by 'revisionists'. Therefore he began the preparations for steering the revolution in China in a new and extremely radical direction.

Mao's decision to launch the Cultural Revolution was driven by a number of motives linked to his main desire to ensure that revolution was continuous and that there was no slipping back into capitalist ideas and behaviours.

▶ **Figure 4.1** Mao's motives in launching the Cultural Revolution

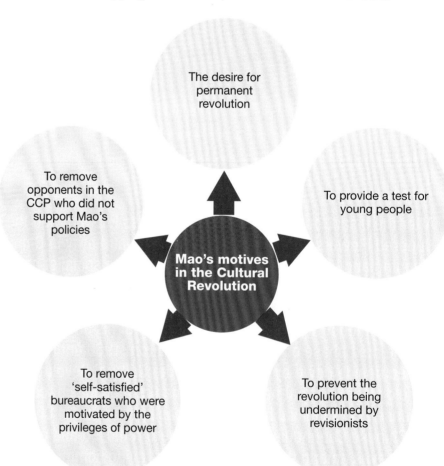

- **The desire for permanent revolution:** Mao was determined that the revolution should not fail, and he wanted to make sure that old attitudes and behaviours did not undo the changes introduced by the CCP since 1949. He was convinced that this was what had happened in the Soviet Union under Khrushchev, and he would not allow it to happen in China too.

- **To provide a test for young people:** Mao believed that the strength of the CCP came from its years of struggle, from the Long March, the war against Japan and the Civil War. Young communists had no experience of this type of struggle, but he believed that it was necessary for them to be involved in struggle in order to identify with the revolution. The Cultural Revolution would allow them to become true revolutionaries.

- **To remove 'self-satisfied' officials who were motivated by the privileges of power:** Mao believed that communist China was being run by bureaucrats who were not interested in revolution but were motivated by the power that they had achieved and the social and economic benefits that accompanied that power. Mao feared that they would grow into a new class of Mandarins (who had dominated the government during the Qing dynasty).

- **To prevent the revolution being weakened by revisionists:** Mao opposed the measures that had been adopted in China after the failure of the Great Leap Forward. He was deeply suspicious that Liu and Deng had encouraged private trade and ownership because they were capitalist sympathisers. He believed that revisionists were to be found in all areas of art, education and culture, and that they needed to be removed to save the revolution.

- **To remove opponents in the CCP who did not support Mao's policies:** Mao feared that he had opponents within the CCP leadership who were seeking to remove him. The Cultural Revolution offered an ideal opportunity to destroy this opposition. His main targets were Liu and Deng.

SOURCE A

Mao swimming in the Yangtze River.

SOURCE B

From an account of Mao's return to politics by Zhisui Li, Mao's personal doctor.

I was in Beijing on July 16, 1966, when Mao took his celebrated swim in the Yangtze River. Having been swimming with Mao so many times before, I barely noticed the event. Nor did it occur to me that foreign sceptics might gasp with disbelief that a seventy-three-year-old man could swim faster and further than an Olympic champion. I knew how swiftly the Yangtze River flows … I also knew by then that Mao's swims were acts of defiance against the party leadership and a signal that the battle was about to begin.

The first sign that Mao was ready to start a Cultural Revolution came in 1965 when Mao forced Wu Han, the deputy mayor of Beijing and an intellectual, to resign. Mao did this because he disapproved of a play that Wu had written that could be interpreted as a criticism of Mao's regime. The following year, in March, Mao established the Central Cultural Revolution Group (CCRG) under the leadership of his fanatical supporter, Chen Boda. The implementation of the Cultural Revolution's policies was dominated by the Maoists Lin Biao (head of the PLA), Jiang Qing (Mao's fourth wife) and Kang Sheng (the head of the secret police).

On 16 July 1966, Mao launched the Cultural Revolution with his much-advertised swim across the Yangtze River. Mao's swim in the Yangtze meant that his exile was over. He was returning to the political stage.

ACTIVITY

Study Source B. Swimming in rivers is not something political leaders usually do. So why do you think Mao carried out the Yangtze swim?

4.2 THE KEY FEATURES OF THE CULTURAL REVOLUTION

LEARNING OBJECTIVES

- Understand the importance of mass mobilisation, young people and the Red Guard
- Understand the use of propaganda, the Cult of Mao and the importance of the Little Red Book
- Understand the role of the PLA and the removal of opponents.

MASS MOBILISATION AND THE ROLE OF YOUNG PEOPLE

One of the most important features of the Cultural Revolution was the way in which Mao mobilised young people to carry out the ideas behind the Cultural Revolution. The first step in this mass mobilisation of the young was on 5 August 1966, when a **big character poster** written by Mao himself was published. He called upon the young to attack the revisionists in the CCP in a 'Bombard the Headquarters' campaign. Young people were encouraged to attack authority and to regard rebellion as a positive force for good.

SOURCE C

Members of the Red Guard fixing big character posters on to a wall in Beijing University.

KEY TERM

big character poster the large posters on which accusations directed at political enemies were painted. They were cheap to produce, often anonymous and effective in spreading ideas

The next stage in mobilising the young was by organising eight mass rallies in Tiananmen Square in Beijing between August and November 1966. The first rally, on 18 August, was the most popular. Over a million young people from across the country arrived in Beijing to see their hero Chairman Mao. The crowds listened to a speech by Mao's closest supporter, Lin Biao, in which they were encouraged to attack not only the leaders of the CCP who had adopted revisionist ideas, but also all aspects of China's culture that could be regarded as 'old'.

THE ATTACK ON THE 'FOUR OLDS'

The eight mass rallies launched the campaign against the 'Four Olds':

- old habits
- old ideas
- old culture
- old customs.

EXTEND YOUR KNOWLEDGE

The young people were so convinced that they needed to carry out a thorough revolution that they wanted to change the traffic signals in China. They claimed that since red was the symbol of revolution, the red traffic light should represent 'go' and not 'stop'. Zhou Enlai had to use all his skills to persuade them to keep the red light. He explained that it symbolised how they were stopping the threat to the revolution. Only this prevented absolute chaos on China's roads.

The young people were encouraged to attack everything in China that was associated with the past. Nothing was considered to be worth preserving. The young people carried out the campaign with great enthusiasm, which shows how they had been thoroughly indoctrinated to follow Mao's instructions. They attacked churches and cultural sites, and invaded people's homes to seize possessions that were associated with the old bourgeoisie including books, jewellery and musical instruments. It was only the presence of the PLA that prevented them from destroying the Forbidden Palace.

THE RED GUARDS AND THE USE OF VIOLENCE

The term 'Red Guard' was first used in May 1966 when students and schoolchildren formed themselves into units to carry out Mao's instructions to attack the opponents of the revolution. They wore a military uniform with a red armband and a leather belt. The leather belt was an essential item; Red Guards used it to whip 'class enemies'. The Red Guards were fanatically loyal to Mao and thoroughly indoctrinated in Mao Zedong Thought.

The number of Red Guard units grew rapidly in August 1966. The first members were the children of party officials. They came from the elite middle schools in China and could claim to have an excellent class background. However, very soon, young people from so-called 'bad-class' backgrounds were allowed to join. They were often the most violent of the Red Guards, because they wanted to prove their loyalty to Chairman Mao. The organisation also allowed young people from all backgrounds to settle old arguments and to get revenge on those who had punished them in the past. Vast numbers of these young people travelled to Beijing to attend one of the mass rallies between August and November 1966, and then carried the message throughout China. This task was made possible by the decision to allow the Red Guards to travel for free on the railways.

▲ **Figure 4.2** Reasons why young people joined the Red Guard

Red Guards parade their victims through the streets wearing dunce hats.

The Red Guard was responsible for the most violent phase of the Cultural Revolution. The members carried out frenzied acts of violence in implementing the attack on the Four Olds. In so-called 'struggle sessions', their victims were forced onto their knees with arms held back in an 'aeroplane' position and were made to confess their crimes. If they resisted, they were beaten and kicked until they submitted.

The Red Guard was able to carry out these acts of violence because they had official approval. Although members of the Red Guard often chose their own victims, there were also occasions when the attacks were direct by the CCRG, most especially by Madame Mao, Jiang Qing. Mao would not call an end to the violence as long as it was effective in removing opponents. Beijing and Shanghai probably saw the worst of the violence, but nowhere was safe. In the years 1966–76, more than 67,000 people were killed in Guangxi province alone.

EXAM-STYLE QUESTION

A01 | **A02**

SKILLS ADAPTIVE LEARNING

Explain **two** causes of the violence that occurred during the Cultural Revolution.

(8 marks)

HINT

This question is about causation. When answering questions about why things happen, good answers will link the identified reasons to the outcome. Write a paragraph explaining each of the reasons that you select.

THE CULT OF MAO AND THE LITTLE RED BOOK

The Cultural Revolution was made possible by the Cult of Mao. This was a personality cult. It gave Mao a special status and involved the worship of Mao. Pictures, busts and statues of Mao appeared everywhere in China, in the streets and public buildings, in factories and schools. Mao held an extraordinary degree of power over young people. They had been brought up to regard him as a god. He was worshipped as the great hero who had saved China from foreign domination (control by foreigners) and brought communism to China. Now the young people were given the task of saving the revolution from the acts of revisionists, and they devoted themselves to the task with unquestioning obedience. Mao was described by the young people as 'the red sun rising in the east', and his teachings were regarded as the absolute truth.

This attitude to Mao had been developed by a careful propaganda campaign that placed Mao above all other CCP leaders. It was most successful among the young people, where mass suggestion and the desire to copy the behaviour of their peers (people of the same age and social position) was most effective. The account by actress Liu Xiaoqing in Source E shows what extreme admiration the young felt for Mao.

SOURCE E

From Liu Xiaoqing's memoirs of her life in China during the Cultural Revolution. Liu's account was written at the height of the Cult of Mao.

Everyone says that you never forget your first love. I can't really say that I ever had a first love, for in my childhood and youth the man I loved and admired most of all was Mao Zedong. I gave him my sincerest love, as well as all my longing and hopes. He was an idol I worshipped with all my heart.

Chairman Mao, you were my first object of desire!

The first song I learnt to sing was 'The East is Red'. When I was a Red Guard I could recite all of his quotations word perfect. My brain was armed with Mao Zedong Thought.

If I ever had any problems I would search Chairman Mao's writings for an answer. When we lost one of our chicks I looked for help in his works. When, not long after, the chick reappeared, I knew it was due to the intercession of our Great, Wise and Correct Chairman Mao.

One of the essential aspects of the cult of Mao was the production and use of the 'Little Red Book'. In 1964, Lin Biao had organised the publication of a collection of Mao's well-known sayings for the PLA. Soon it became a vital element of the Cultural Revolution. Every Red Guard had one and used it as guidance for their behaviour. As Liu Xiaoqing said, it was believed to have an almost religious power, and many people believed that it could work miracles. There were accounts printed in the newspapers of the blind being able to see and the disabled being able to walk as a result of the Little Red Book.

It was not just the Little Red Book that was an essential possession. The production of Mao souvenirs became a huge business, and no home was complete without a portrait or model of Mao. The sale of badges to pin on hats and clothing increased. One young man even made a hole in his chest where he could pin his badge, so that Mao would be close to his heart.

The Little Red Book with the image of Mao Zedong on the front. During the Cultural Revolution, 750 million copies were distributed in China.

EDUCATION

EXTEND YOUR KNOWLEDGE

The badge-making industry in China became very successful. People purchased hundreds of badges in a desire to demonstrate their loyalty to Chairman Mao. Demand was so great that the production of badges used up all of China's supplies of aluminium. In 1969, Mao himself was forced to step in and stop production. The production of badges damaged the aircraft industry, because it could not get the supplies of aluminium to build planes.

The importance of young people to the Cultural Revolution made it unavoidable that the education system would be involved in the events. Indeed, as intellectuals were identified as enemies in the attack on the Four Olds, it was certain that children would turn against their teachers as reactionaries who had been holding back the progress to communism. The Revolution began in the university town of Qinghua, where Red Guard units were first formed in May 1966. It soon spread from the university students to involve children in colleges and schools. By the end of the year, all schools and colleges were closed so that children could take part in the revolutionary struggle. Their first victims were their teachers. Many were tortured and beaten to death, while others sought to escape this fate by committing suicide. Historian Frank Dikötter describes the attack on teachers in Beijing in August 1966 in Extract A.

ACTIVITY

1 Create a large spider diagram summarising the key elements of the Cult of Mao.
2 Explain why so many young people believed in the Cult of Mao.
3 Write a detailed account of the impact of the Cultural Revolution on the lives of young people in 1966. Did all young people have the same experience?

EXTRACT A

A description of the treatment of teachers in a book on the Cultural Revolution published in 2016.

A wave of violence engulfed the capital after the rally on Tiananmen Square. At the Beijing Third Girls Middle School, the principal was beaten to death. The dean hanged herself. At another middle school near Beijing Normal University the principal was ordered to stand under the hot sun while Red Guards poured boiling water over him. New depths of horror were plumbed at another middle school, this one attached to the Beijing Teachers' College, as a biology teacher was knocked to the ground, beaten and dragged by her legs through the front door and down the steps, her head bumping against the concrete. She died after being further tormented for several hours. Then the other teachers, rounded up as so many monsters and demons, were forced to take turns and beat her dead body. At elementary schools, where the students were no older than thirteen, some teachers were made to swallow nails and excrement, others had their heads shaved and were forced to slap each other.

THE PLA AND THE END OF THE VIOLENCE

Mao had encouraged the use of violence by the Red Guard. He even told them that disorder and chaos were good. However, by January 1967, China had fallen into near-anarchy. The Red Guards turned against one another, and attacked the workers' units that had been formed to drive the Cultural Revolution in the factories. All this worried the PLA. The army was concerned that the continued radicalism of the Red Guard would soon turn it against the PLA. Military leaders did not want the army to be forced to make confessions and take part in struggle sessions like the other party members. Therefore, they were anxious to take control of the Cultural Revolution from the Red Guard.

At first, Mao would not become involved. However, by September 1967, even he was concerned by the behaviour of the Red Guards. He feared that the anarchy weakened China and that foreign powers might take advantage of the situation and seize Chinese territory. In 1968, Mao ordered the military to destroy the Red Guards and regain control. The PLA closed down the Red Guard newspapers and reopened the schools to encourage young people to leave the streets and return to education. The PLA also conducted a bloody **purge** of the Red Guards. Thousands were killed, a feature of the Cultural Revolution that became very clear to foreign powers when bodies began to appear on the shores of the British-held island of Hong Kong, which is situated downriver from Guangdong province.

KEY TERM

purge the 'removal' of opponents

THE 'UP TO THE MOUNTAINS AND DOWN TO THE VILLAGES' CAMPAIGN

The most violent phase of the Cultural Revolution had been brought to an end by the spring of 1969. There was now a problem of what to do with the millions of radicalised young people who had flooded into the cities to lead the revolution. Mao wanted to end their violent behaviour in the towns and cities. Therefore, the party now encouraged a new revolutionary experience for the young. They were to head for the countryside, to learn how the peasants lived. Mao never stopped believing that the peasants were the centre of the communist revolution, and the young people were now to be educated in the realities of rural life. This would also bring them more effectively under the control of the PLA, because the military ran a large number of the communes in the country. Figure 4.3 summarises the main reasons why Mao launched the 'up to the mountains and down to the villages' campaign.

▶ **Figure 4.3** Reasons for the 'up to the mountains and down to the villages' campaign

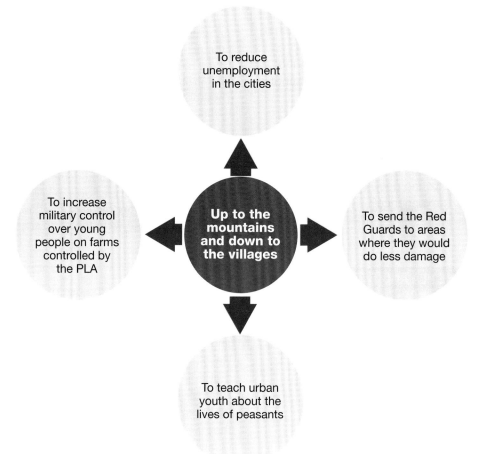

EXTRACT B

The recollections of a member of the Red Guard who went to work on a communal farm during the Cultural Revolution.

The days were long, so long. The work was endless. At five in the morning we were cutting the oil-bearing plants. The black seeds rolled on to my neck and into my shoes as I laid the plants down. I did not bother to wipe the sweat that was dripping and salted my eyes. I did not have the time… When we worked, we were sunk into the sea of the plants. We barely straightened our backs. We had no time to straighten our backs… Yan [the person in charge] was a horse-rider. We were her horses. She did not have to whip us to get us moving. We felt the chill of a whip on the back when she walked by and examined our work.

The vast majority of young people did not enjoy peasant life. The work was difficult and the standards of living were low. The peasants did not welcome the extra mouths to feed, because they had not been given additional rations for the newcomers.

The millions of young people who were forced into the countryside were thoroughly disillusioned by the campaign. The experience led them to question the authority of the party and their faith in Mao. Many of them believed that they had been used in the power struggle in the party.

ACTIVITY

1 Study Extract B. Explain why young people found life in the countryside to be very hard.
2 Working with a partner, write two lists: one listing the role and activities of young people in the early years of the Cultural Revolution (1966–69), the second listing their role and activities from 1969 onwards.
3 Discuss with your partner the ways in which the young people's lives changed. How would the changes affect their support for Chairman Mao?

THE REMOVAL OF THE OPPOSITION TO MAO IN THE COMMUNIST PARTY

One reason why Mao had started the Cultural Revolution was because he believed that many members of the CCP were revisionists who had become too fond of power and good living, and were preventing the revolution from progressing. He wanted to remove these people by purging the party. The Red Guard played an important role in this. They attacked the party cadres, who were accused of acting more like capitalists than communists. The purge was highly successful. By 1969, more than 70 per cent of the provincial and regional party officials and 60 per cent of the highest-level officials in the national party had been removed. They were replaced by members of the PLA that now became very powerful in the CCP. This suited Mao very well, because the new members of the Central Committee were fanatically devoted to him.

Mao also wanted to remove the leading members of the CCP who he believed were ignoring him as he got older, and because he did not agree with the economic policies that they had implemented after the Great Leap Forward. He identified Liu Shaoqi, the head of the state, and Deng Xiaoping, a leading member of the Politburo, as his greatest enemies. In the Party Conference in October 1966, Mao criticised Liu and forced him to confess to betraying the revolution. Liu was attacked in the press as a 'big scab' and a traitor. He was arrested and imprisoned. In 1969 he died of the lung disease pneumonia, in an unheated prison cell. Mao had refused to allow him to be treated in hospital.

SOURCE G

From an article in a Beijing newspaper published in January 1969. The article was entitled 'Big scab Liu Shaoqi is the mortal foe of the working class'.

During the last few decades... the big scab Liu Shaoqi engaged in deception and blackmail everywhere and committed countless crimes... He is the mortal foe of the working class ... He always opposed Chairman Mao's great teachings on carrying out large-scale mass movements in factories and mines...

The arch scab Liu Shaoqi's numerous crimes of suppressing the workers' movement before and after liberation prove him to be a top spy sent by the Chiang Kai-shek regime into the ranks of the working class.

SOURCE H

A statue of Chairman Mao in Lijiang, China.

Deng Xiaoping was luckier than Liu. He was forced out of office, but he had the support of Zhou Enlai. He therefore survived the era of the Cultural Revolution and rose to the top office after Mao's death.

When the purges were taking place, Lin Biao lost Mao's support. The PLA that he controlled had restored order, but in the process Lin had become very powerful. Lin was accepted as Mao's successor. Mao now became suspicious that Lin was planning to overthrow him and set up a military dictatorship. Lin and his son attempted to escape from China in 1971, but both died when the plane in which they were travelling ran out of fuel and crashed. It has been said that Zhou Enlai had prevented it from refuelling.

EXAM-STYLE QUESTION

A01 **A02**

Explain **two** ways in which the treatment of party members in the Cultural Revolution was similar to their treatment in the anti-Rightist campaigns of the 1950s.

(6 marks)

HINT

This question is about comparison. You should identify two similarities and give some details to explain in what way the features were similar. You will need to refresh your memory about the anti-rightist campaign from Chapter 3.

4.3 THE IMPACT OF THE CULTURAL REVOLUTION ON CHINA AND MAO'S POSITION

LEARNING OBJECTIVES

- Understand the impact of the Cultural Revolution on Mao's position
- Understand the impact of the Cultural Revolution on China's economy
- Understand the impact of the Cultural Revolution on the lives of ordinary people in China.

THE IMPACT OF THE CULTURAL REVOLUTION ON MAO'S POSITION

The Cultural Revolution had a very significant impact on Mao's own position. He had become much more powerful as a result of the events of the Cultural Revolution. He had always believed that transforming China into a communist country required absolute obedience to the leader, and the Cultural Revolution largely achieved this. Mao's opponents had been removed and this made him an unchallenged leader. The CCP was firmly under Mao's control. Those party members who had questioned Mao in the past had been replaced by loyal members who were devoted to him. The population gave their absolute support to him. This loyalty had been achieved by the establishment of prison camps known as **laogi**, where opponents were 're-educated' to support Mao and the ideals of communism. The very difficult conditions, the planned starvation and use of torture ensured that those who survived the experience and were released would never criticise the regime again.

KEY TERM

laogi labour camps established for the re-education of opponents to Mao's regime. Many were built in the most hostile and inhospitable regions of China

The events of the Cultural Revolution increased Mao's power. They also increased his suspicions so that he came to believe that leading members of the CCP were making plans against him. This can be seen in the fall of Lin Biao (see page 76). Thus, as the Cultural Revolution ended, Mao was quite isolated at the top of the political system. His health was also rapidly declining, and he was seldom seen in public.

THE IMPACT OF THE CULTURAL REVOLUTION ON CHINA'S ECONOMY

The Cultural Revolution had a negative effect on the development of the Chinese economy. Managers whose loyalty to communism was suspect were removed and their replacements often lacked the necessary skills to run successful businesses. Even when they were skilled, the use of trains to transport Red Guards around the country meant there was a shortage of trains to bring raw materials to the factories and transport goods to market. The worst years were between 1966 and 1970, when industrial production fell by 13 per cent. The production of essential materials fell dramatically:

- coal production declined from 260 million tonnes to 206 million tonnes
- oil production declined from 15 million tonnes to 13.9 million tonnes
- steel production fell from 15 million tonnes to 1 million tonnes.

This was very bad news for an economy that was only just emerging from the effects of the Great Leap Forward. The impact on agriculture was less severe, because the Cultural Revolution was essentially an urban movement. However, grain production fell and the government had to introduce rationing.

There were improvements after 1969. The end of the Cultural Revolution allowed production to expand once more, but progress overall was very slow for a country that was supposed to be focused on rapid modernisation.

▶ **Figure 4.4** Graph showing the decline in production in the years 1966–70

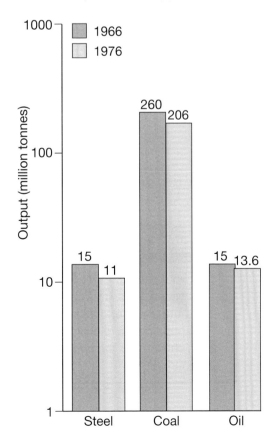

THE IMPACT OF THE CULTURAL REVOLUTION ON THE LIVES OF THE CHINESE PEOPLE

The Cultural Revolution affected the Chinese population in many areas of their ordinary lives as follows.

▼ AREA	▼ EFFECTS
Education	There was a huge impact on education. In the years 1966–70, schools were closed because it was seen as more important to train young people to be loyal party members than to educate them. The consequences of this were made clear in 1982, when the **census** revealed that less than 1 per cent of the population had a degree. Even more shocking was the fact that only 35 per cent of the population had attended school up to the age of 12.
Family	The Cultural Revolution weakened the family, which was criticised as one of the Four Olds. Children were taught to look to Mao and the CCP before their parents. They were encouraged to report on their parents if they saw any signs of support for the old way of life. Although it proved difficult to remove centuries of belief in the wisdom of the elders, the removal of so many young people to the villages meant that family ties were broken.
Health	The progress that had been made in training doctors and in improving healthcare during the 1950s was damaged by the Cultural Revolution. Doctors were suspected by the party as being reactionaries who were more interested in achieving a comfortable life than in serving the revolution. Many feared they would be accused of opposing the Cultural Revolution, so they cancelled operations and showed solidarity with hospital workers by spending their time sweeping floors. On a positive note, the rapid training of so-called 'barefoot doctors', who completed a short practical course and then went to provide health care in the most rural villages in China, did lead to significant improvements in the lives of peasants.
Religion	Religion was criticised as one of the Four Olds. All public worship was forbidden and clergy (priests) were rounded up and sent to prison camps. There were campaigns against Confucianism which, it was claimed, had prevented China from modernising. In spite of the attacks, it proved surprisingly difficult to wipe out religion. Some clergy were able to carry on in secret, and ancestor worship returned later.
Culture	Jiang Qing, Mao's fourth wife, was put in charge of developing a new Communist-approved culture and removing traditional Chinese culture. She took on the task with enthusiasm. She was responsible for introducing a system of strict censorship. Artists were too scared of being arrested to be creative. China was reduced to a cultural desert where nothing of great artistic value was produced.

EXTEND YOUR KNOWLEDGE

Madam Mao, Jiang Qing, was Mao's fourth wife. She was a former actress and had a great interest in the arts. She played a leading role in the Cultural Revolution as the person in charge of the Central Cultural Revolution Group. She ordered that operas and ballets must have revolutionary themes in order to transform China's culture. She promoted some writers who are famous today, such as Anchee Min.

Jiang Qing was so revolutionary in her ideas about art and beauty that she encouraged children to pull the heads off flowers to show that they despised the bourgeois concept of beauty.

EXTEND YOUR KNOWLEDGE

Doctors stopped using anaesthetics and other painkillers during the Cultural Revolution. It was believed that a good revolutionary would bear pain without reacting, whereas a reactionary would cry out with pain.

ACTIVITY

1 To what extent did Mao achieve absolute control over China during the years 1966–76? Draw up a table with two columns: one for control and the other for challenges to his rule. Review the information in this chapter and list relevant examples on each column in the table.
2 Which side has the strongest evidence? Write a paragraph giving your judgement.

4.4 THE EFFECT OF THE SINO–SOVIET SPLIT ON THE CHINESE ECONOMY

LEARNING OBJECTIVES

- Understand the reasons for the Sino–Soviet split
- Understand the impact the Sino–Soviet split had on the Chinese economy
- Understand the continued deterioration of Sino–Soviet relations during the Cultural Revolution.

The relationship between China and the Soviet Union had been a difficult one since the Communists took charge in China. Although Mao knew it was useful to China to work with the strongest communist power in the world, he was always suspicious of the intentions of the Soviets. This suspicion increased significantly after Khrushchev had denounced Stalin in 1956 (see Chapter 3, page 60). Economic aid from the Soviet Union had been valuable at the beginning of China's modernisation programme. In 1958, the Soviet Union had sent more than 10,000 economic and military advisers to China, as well as providing training for Chinese technicians in the Soviet Union, and this had allowed the Chinese to make rapid progress in industrialisation. However, Mao believed that the support made China too dependent on the Soviet Union. So, in the late 1950s, he announced that China needed to be independent in its economic development. He called this 'walking on two legs'.

The relationship worsened rapidly in the early 1960s. In April 1960, Mao accused the Soviet Union of being a revisionist country when its leaders began to develop friendly relations with the United States of America. Meanwhile, Khrushchev criticised the Great Leap Forward. Tensions increased on the Sino–Soviet borders and Mao feared that the Soviet Union might launch an invasion of China.

In 1960, Khrushchev took back the Soviet technicians and military experts, who had continued to increase since 1958. This affected China's economy, as it had relied on these experts for their economic knowledge while it was training its own experts. It was particularly damaging as the advisers had been helping China to overcome the economic crisis brought about by the Great Leap Forward. The Soviet Union had assisted China in building 156 major industrial plants, which included iron and steel works and power stations. When the Soviets left, over 200 projects were cancelled. The impact on the weapons programme was potentially the most damaging. As they left, the Soviets destroyed all the documents relating to nuclear energy, and this caused a setback to the nuclear programme in China.

EXTEND YOUR KNOWLEDGE

The Cuban Missile Crisis was a disagreement between the USA and the Soviet Union in October 1962. The USA had discovered a nuclear site on the island of Cuba, off the coast of Florida, and that the Soviet Union was shipping nuclear missiles to Cuba. After a 13-day disagreement, Khrushchev ordered the Soviet ships to return to the Soviet Union.

The final split came in 1962. Mao used the Cuban Missile Crisis to accuse Khrushchev of cowardice, while Khrushchev claimed that Mao's policies would lead to nuclear war.

As a consequence of losing Soviet support, China was forced to seek friends elsewhere. This came at a high price. China provided loans of US$2 billion to African nations to secure their support. Communism held a great attraction for the developing African nations which had been freed from imperial rule. Mao

ACTIVITY

Write a short newspaper article explaining in what ways the Sino–Soviet split affected China's economy.

wanted to ensure that they preferred China to the Soviet Union. He argued that Chinese communism, with its focus on the peasantry, was more appropriate to Africa than Soviet communism, with its emphasis on the industrial working class. However, in spite of the loss of Soviet aid, and the cost of seeking new friendships, China was able to continue with its nuclear programme. The destroyed documents were recreated, and China tested its own nuclear weapon in 1964 and its own **H-bomb** in 1967.

SOURCE I

Visitors at the museum at the site of China's first nuclear weapons base in Haiyan county, Qinghai province.

The years of the Cultural Revolution were characterised by a further worsening of Sino–Soviet relations. In part, the Cultural Revolution was carried out to prevent the growth of Chinese communism from being weakened by bureaucracy – as had happened in the Soviet Union. When President Khrushchev was replaced by President Brezhnev in 1964, Mao claimed that there was no change in the Soviet Union's government – that it was Khrushchevism without Khrushchev, and that this meant the Soviets were still following the path of revisionism. This view was strengthened in 1967, when Red Guards attacked the Soviet embassy in Beijing and intimidated Soviet officials. In 1969, Lin Biao accused the Soviet leaders of being **social fascists**. The bad feeling between China and the Soviet Union was seen in a number of border disagreements. In 1969, there were a series of border fights on China's north-western frontier in Xinjiang. An all-out war was avoided when the two

KEY TERM

social fascist a term that was first used by Stalin to denounce those Communists who were prepared to compromise with their political enemies

sides agreed to have talks, but Mao then came to believe that the greatest threat to China was not the capitalist West but the Soviet Union. This led to two actions.

■ In the 1970s, Mao tried to improve China's relations with the USA. In 1972, he invited the American president Richard Nixon to China for talks, and agreed on the development of cultural, educational and economic relations.

■ China's nuclear weapons were now aimed not at the USA, but the Soviet Union.

▶ **Figure 4.5** The Sino–Soviet split and its impact: stages in the decline of China's relationship with the Soviet Union

1958
More than 10,000 Soviet economic and military advisers sent to China

April 1960
Mao accuses the Soviet Union of being a revisionist country

1960
Khrushchev recalled the Soviet advisers from China

1962
Mao used the Cuban Missile Crisis to accuse Krushchev of cowardice

1964
Mao claimed that the new Soviet leader Brezhnev was also a revisionist

1969
Lin Biao claimed the Soviet leaders were social fascists

EXAM-STYLE QUESTION

A01 **A02**

SKILLS   PROBLEM SOLVING, REASONING, DECISION MAKING

How far did family life change in China in the years 1949–76?

You may use the following in your answer:
■ the 1950 Marriage Law
■ the impact of the Cultural Revolution 1966–76 on education.
You **must** also use information of your own.   **(16 marks)**

HINT

This question is about change. When writing about change, you will need to go beyond description. You will need to give examples of what is different about family life by 1976 compared to 1949. You should also write at least one paragraph about what stayed the same. You will need to refresh your memory about the 1950 Marriage Law from Chapter 3. Remember to bring in another topic of your own choosing, to look at changes to family life.

RECAP

RECALL QUESTIONS

1 What action did Mao take which marked the beginning of the Cultural Revolution?
2 What were the Four Olds?
3 List three characteristics of a typical Red Guard.
4 How were the accused treated in struggle sessions?
5 What use was made of the Little Red Book?
6 List two ways in which education was affected by the Cultural Revolution.
7 Why were young people disillusioned by the 'up to the mountains and down to the villages' campaign?
8 Which leading member of the CCP was arrested and imprisoned by Mao?
9 What was the effect of the Cultural Revolution on culture?
10 Why did Sino–Soviet relations break down by 1962?

CHECKPOINT

STRENGTHEN
S1 Write a paragraph describing the actions of young people in the Cultural Revolution.
S2 Why did the PLA become involved in the Cultural Revolution, and what was the result?
S3 List three ways in which the Cultural Revolution was damaging to China's modernisation programme.

CHALLENGE
C1 Do you think that there were any positive results from the Cultural Revolution?
C2 Explain how Lin Biao's position changed during the Cultural Revolution.
C3 Do you think Mao was a successful leader of China? Make a list with three columns: one for his aims, one for successes and one for failures. Did he mostly succeed in his aims or mostly fail? Write a paragraph giving your judgement.

SUMMARY

- Mao launched the Cultural Revolution because he wanted to save the revolution from revisionists and to remove his opponents.
- Mao mobilised young people to carry out the Cultural Revolution because he believed they needed to be tested and because they were easiest to indoctrinate.
- The Red Guard was the main revolutionary force. It was used to attack the Four Olds, and was responsible for closing down the schools and forcing so-called opponents into struggle sessions to confess crimes.
- The Red Guard was inspired by the Cult of Mao and his ideas as contained in the Little Red Book.
- Mao used the PLA to destroy the Red Guard when the violence in the cities turned into anarchy.
- Young people became disillusioned with Mao when they were sent to the villages and mountains to learn about the lives of the peasants.
- Mao used the Cultural Revolution to remove leading members of the CCP and to get absolute control over the party.
- The Cultural Revolution resulted in significant declines in education and industrial output, and weakened traditional institutions such as the family and religion.
- The Sino–Soviet split led to the removal of Soviet experts from China and the cancellation of economic projects, but by the mid-1960s, China had managed to produce its own nuclear weapons.

EXAM GUIDANCE: PART (C) QUESTIONS

A01 **A02**

SKILLS PROBLEM SOLVING, REASONING,
DECISION MAKING

Question to be answered: How far did the lives of peasants in China change in the years 1934–62?

You may use the following in your answer:
- treatment of peasants by the GMD
- the Great Famine.

You **must** also use information of your own.

(16 marks)

1 **Analysis Question 1: What is the question type testing?**
In this question you have to demonstrate that you have knowledge and understanding of the ways that the lives of peasants in China changed in the years 1934–62. You also have to reach a judgement on the extent of that change.

2 **Analysis Question 2: What do I have to do to answer the question well?**
- You have been given two factors on which to write. You don't have to use them and can provide your own factors. (But it seems sensible to do so!)
- However, you must avoid just giving the information. What changes did these events cause?
- You are also asked 'how far' the lives of peasants in China changed. So when discussing these events, you need to consider whether the lives of peasants in China changed or whether the evidence suggests it mainly stayed the same.
- You will also see that the question says you must use information of your own. So that should include at least one factor, other than those you have been given.
- That factor might be the Agrarian Land Reform.

3 **Analysis Question 3: Are there any techniques I can use to make it very clear that I am doing what is needed to be successful?**
You will be up against time pressures so here are some useful techniques that might help you succeed.
- Don't write a lengthy introduction. Give a brief introduction which answers the question straight away and shows what your paragraphs are going to be about.
- To make sure you stay focused on the question and avoid just writing narrative, try to use the words of the question at the beginning of each paragraph.

Answer

Here is a student response to the question. The teacher has made some comments. Rewrite the section where comments are made to improve it.

Good introduction with a clear focus on the question.

There were many changes in the lives of peasants in China in the years 1934-62. They were not treated well by Chiang Kai-shek who needed them in his army. They were promised much more when Mao became leader of China because he believed that the communist revolution would begin in the countryside and he also wanted to encourage more peasants to go to the towns and become industrial workers. Not all of the changes were positive though, so some peasants may have thought that there was not much real change.

This is a great paragraph. It has an opening sentence which explains what the paragraph is about – the point of the paragraph – and it then uses detailed knowledge to support the point. And you have considered 'how far' by showing that the changes were different in the communist areas! Well done!

The lives of peasants did change while the GMD were in power and the changes made their lives much more difficult. One very important change happened when the GMD were trying to stop the Communists from escaping during the Long March. The peaceful life of the peasants was disturbed by the GMD troops that marched through their villages and took the resources they needed to feed their army. This happened again during the Civil War in 1945-49. In fact it was much worse because now Chiang and his men forced peasants to join the GMD army (NRA). Thousands of conscripted peasants died from their treatment. So we can see that life got much worse for the peasants while Chiang was in power. He treated them cruelly and did nothing about the rich landlords who charged them high rents and kept them in poverty. However, during this period, peasants who lived in communist controlled areas were treated much better. Mao had rules about treating peasants with respect. He also brought in rent controls which improved life for peasants.

Another good paragraph. You answer the question, give contextual knowledge and develop the changes well. You have also considered 'how far' when you look at the seizure of land as part of a collectivisation programme.

There were very many changes that were introduced when Mao became the leader of China. Mao wanted to modernise agriculture so that more people could move to the towns and become industrial workers. Before Mao came to power, there were rich peasants who owned land and were landlords. Other peasants had no land and had to work for landlords. In 1950 in the Agrarian Reform Law, the land was taken away from the landlords and given to the peasants. This was a big change and very popular. Many landlords were denounced and about a million were executed. This change which gave the peasants their own land did not last long though, because from the mid-1950s Mao introduced collectivisation. The collectivisation programme took the land away from peasants and gave it to the state. Millions of peasants were forced to join the collectives which they did not like. The state owned the land and they worked for the state so it was similar to when they had had to work for landlords.

Another very good paragraph with a focus on change and relevant examples used as evidence. You could improve this by referring to some continuities. The peasants suffered with starvation under Chiang, although this was on a much greater scale. You could also look at continuities and change in farming methods.

Finally, the lives of peasants changed because of the Great Famine. Millions of peasants lost their lives because Mao seized food from the collectives to feed the workers in the towns and because the peasants had no incentive to work hard when they would not gain any profits from the food they produced. This meant that production went down. About 50 million people died in China. The people who suffered most were the peasants in Tibet where they were forced to change from growing barley to growing wheat and corn but the land was not suitable so the crops failed.

It is a shame there was not time for a brief conclusion.

What are the strengths and weaknesses of this answer?

You can see the strengths and weaknesses of this answer from what the teacher says. If all three paragraphs had dealt with both change and continuity and the conclusion had developed explanation, this would have been an excellent answer.

Work with a friend

Discuss with a friend how you write a conclusion to finish this answer.

Are there any other parts of it you could improve?

5. CHINA, 1976–89

LEARNING OBJECTIVES

■ Understand the rise and fall of the Gang of Four

■ Understand the changes introduced under Deng Xiaoping in society and in the economy

■ Understand Deng's opposition to political reform and its consequences.

In the years after Mao's death, China underwent considerable change. In 1976, many people had expected Mao to be succeeded by the most enthusiastic supporters of the Cultural Revolution, the Gang of Four, led by Mao's fourth wife Jiang Qing. However, it was in fact Deng Xiaoping, previously denounced as having revisionist ideas, who became the undisputed leader by 1978. In the years 1978–89, Deng presided over a programme of economic modernisation. The result was that some of the key elements of communist economic theory were dropped, and capitalist ideas such as the profit motive and international trade were allowed to return to economic planning. However, in politics, Deng remained a confirmed Communist. He opposed the development of democratic ideas that were increasingly voiced by students. This culminated in the violent repression of the protest in Tiananmen in June 1989.

5.1 THE RISE AND FALL OF THE GANG OF FOUR

LEARNING OBJECTIVES

■ Understand the reasons for the rise of the Gang of Four

■ Understand the reasons for the fall of the Gang of Four

■ Understand why Deng Xiaoping became the leader of China by 1978.

Mao had been the leader of the CCP since the Long March, and by the mid-1970s it was clear that he was nearing the end of his life. This led to a struggle for power in the party as rivals fought to secure the **succession**. It was at this time that the Gang of Four became important.

SOURCE A

The Gang of Four: Zhang Chungqiao, Wang Hangwen, Yao Wenyuan and Jiang Qing.

Zhang Chungqiao	He was originally a journalist. He was a member of the Cultural Revolution Group and became a leading member of the Politburo in 1973.
Wang Hangwen	He had an excellent class background as a worker-peasant and a soldier. He had risen to power in Shanghai in 1967, and in 1973 he was chosen as Mao's successor.
Yao Wenyuan	He came from a socialist background. He was a literary critic and worked in the Office of Propaganda.
Jiang Qing	She was Mao's fourth wife and the leader of the Gang of Four. Her power came from her role as the 'purifier of culture' in the Cultural Revolution. She had a strong support base in Shanghai.

The rise of the Gang of Four began during the Cultural Revolution, when Jiang Qing launched the anti-Confucius campaign. On the outside, this was a campaign against revisionists and to promote communist ideas and practices. However, under the surface, it was used as an attack on Zhou Enlai and Deng Xiaoping. Jiang and her supporters were afraid that Zhou or Deng might become leader after Mao's death.

At first, Mao supported Jiang and her campaign because he wanted to preserve the achievements of the Cultural Revolution. He listened to their criticisms that Deng was a '**capitalist-roader**', and in April 1976, Deng was removed from his posts in the party.

As a consequence of Deng's fall in April 1976 and Zhou Enlai's death in January 1976, the Gang of Four believed that they would take control when Mao died. However, this was not to be the case. When Deng was removed, Mao promoted Hua Guofeng to premier of the PRC and vice-chairman of the CCP. This meant that the Gang of Four had a rival for the leadership. Hua had the support of key military officials and more members of the Politburo than the Gang of Four did. Jiang Qing was very unpopular with the majority of the Politburo, who had objected to her behaviour during the Cultural Revolution.

The Gang of Four was cleverly tricked by the opposition. The members were invited to a Politburo meeting but given different times. When each male member turned up individually, he was arrested. Jiang was arrested at her house before she left for the meeting.

The Gang of Four were put on trial in 1980–81. They were accused of attempting to overthrow the communist state. There was a long list of crimes that the Gang of Four were accused of committing, including the following:
- In 1966, the Gang of Four planned to use the Red Guard to remove Liu Shaoqi and Deng Xiaoping.
- The Gang of Four was accused of plotting to take control because they feared that Mao would bring Deng back from exile. If Deng returned, then the Gang of Four would lose their power, so they told Mao that Zhou and Deng were planning to take power from Mao.
- The Gang of Four punished and tortured opponents. In particular, Jiang was accused of torturing artists who did not agree with her ideas on culture.

At the end of the trial, all four members were found guilty. Jiang and Zhang received death sentences, although these were reduced to life imprisonment. The arrest and trial of the Gang of Four removed the opposition, so Hua Guofeng might have thought that he would definitely become the leader. However, this was not the case. The Politburo really thought of him as a caretaker or temporary leader. Over the next 2 years, the real leader emerged: Deng Xiaoping.

Deng had been removed from his posts but not expelled from the party. He had much support in the party and the military. He had played an important role in organising the recovery from the Great Famine in the early 1960s, and in the 1970s he had played a key part in planning a major programme of industrial growth. He had also accompanied Zhou Enlai on his many foreign missions, so Deng had played an important role in helping to develop China's foreign policy. Therefore, from 1976 to 1978 Deng played a clever waiting game in which he secured military support and developed his role within the party. His position as **paramount leader** of China was confirmed in October 1978.

5.2 ECONOMIC CHANGE UNDER DENG XIAOPING

LEARNING OBJECTIVES

- Understand the changes in agriculture and industry
- Understand the changes in education
- Understand the reasons for and effects of the policy of birth control.

SOURCE B

Deng Xiaoping at the Communist Party Congress, 1977.

Deng was a realist in terms of economic planning. He had gained considerable experience in his work to overcome the Great Famine in the 1960s and in managing economic planning in the early 1970s. He refused to be tied to communist beliefs if they did not work. One of his favourite sayings was: 'It does not matter whether a cat is black or white so long as it catches mice.' His aims were:

- to modernise the Chinese economy
- to develop trade with the outside world
- to encourage foreign investment into China.

Under Mao, Deng's ideas would have been seen as revisionist and therefore suspect. However, now that Mao was gone, he was able to put them into practice with some considerable success.

CHANGES IN AGRICULTURE

The reform of agriculture under Mao had removed the oppressive landlords of the imperial and nationalist eras, but the programme of collectivisation had failed to increase the amount of food produced to the levels needed to allow a shift of population from the countryside to the city. Without a profit motive, the communes had tended to produce only what they needed to feed their members. This was all to change under Deng.

The commune was replaced by the xiang, which was the original village or township. The land was rented by the state to farmers for a period of 15 years. Each xiang had a quota of produce that it had to supply to the state, but the individual famers were allowed to sell any extra produce and any goods that they produced by setting up family craft businesses for a profit at the market. The new system was called the 'household responsibility system'. It was popular with farmers because they were now rewarded for their own work and skills, and they could make themselves much richer than before. This provided the incentive that had been missing, and agricultural production increased to record levels. By 1984, 98 per cent of agricultural households were part of the household responsibility system. One other important change in agriculture was that farmers were allowed to concentrate on growing the type of crop which grew best in their area, instead of having to grow rice and wheat, as they had been made to do under Mao.

▶ **Figure 5.1** A graph showing the increases in grain production, 1978–89

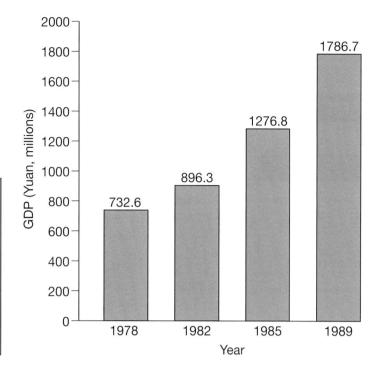

ACTIVITY

1 What do you think Deng meant when he said, 'It does not matter whether a cat is black or white so long as it catches mice'? Explain your answer.

2 Study Figure 5.1. What can you learn from it about Deng's policies?

EXAM-STYLE QUESTION

AO1 **AO2**

SKILLS PROBLEM SOLVING, REASONING, DECISION MAKING

How far did the management of agriculture change in the years 1949–89?

You may use the following in your answer:
■ the establishment of Agricultural Producers Co-operatives (APCs) in 1951–53
■ the role of the xiang under Deng Xiaoping 1978–89.
You **must** also use information of your own. **(16 marks)**

HINT

This question is about changes and continuities over time. When explaining 'how far' something has changed, you need to identify what changed in the methods employed and also those aspects that stayed the same. You have been given two suggestions to help you consider how far the methods used changed. You will also need to make use of at least one example of your own. To complete this task, you will need to refresh your memory of Mao's policy towards agriculture in Chapter 3.

CHANGES IN EDUCATION

The development of a highly educated workforce was one of the key elements in Deng's modernisation programme. Modernisation meant a new approach to education. Although reforms had been introduced in the 1950s, the Cultural Revolution had undone much of the progress made. By 1979, less than 6 per cent of the population had been educated to degree level. Deng's policy was to change this. Industrial progress required technical expertise and a major change in China's higher education system. From 1978, the following policy was put into action.
■ University entrance exams were reintroduced.
■ Private universities were allowed.
■ Chinese students were encouraged to travel to the West for university education.
■ Research institutes that had been closed during the Cultural Revolution were reopened, and their technical staff were reinstated.

The purpose of these reforms was to train a million technical students, who would then use their skills to modernise industrial processes in China. Students who had studied abroad would bring back their knowledge of Western technology and methods of manufacture.

CHANGES IN INDUSTRY

Deng believed that China's economy would benefit by adopting a number of capitalist practices, such as allowing private profit and co-operating with foreign investors. However, he did not entirely abandon central planning, and he kept the state-owned enterprises or businesses (SOEs). But managers and experts now had more freedom to make decisions about targets and profits. Deng adopted an **open door policy** for trade, and encouraged competition with foreign companies as a way of helping Chinese businesses to produce goods of a higher quality, and not just cheaper than those produced in the West.

Deng introduced new Special Economic Zones (SEZs), firstly in coastal areas, where they could easily access the market in Hong Kong and Taiwan. At first, foreign investment was encouraged only in the export industries, but it was so successful that from 1984, Deng allowed foreign investment in home industries and especially in the developing high technology industries. The SEZs enjoyed great success. By the 1990s, China's export trade had grown by 500 per cent. This was helped by giving exporters special tax concessions and freedom from some financial restrictions. Deng was also impressed by the skills of the new, young managerial class that took advantage of the freedoms allowed in Deng's economic system, allowing them to introduce incentives such as bonuses to workers going above their targets.

▶ **Figure 5.2** A graph showing the improvements in manufacturing output, 1978–89

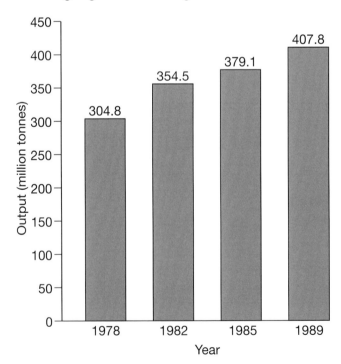

Industrial modernisation was not without its problems. Some workers in the SOEs were unhappy about changing their working practices. Under Mao's system, they were guaranteed a wage regardless of their output. This was known as an 'iron rice bowl'. They knew that they would be able to feed their family. Now Deng wanted incomes to be based on performance. He reduced the subsidies to SOEs because they were supposed to make a profit and fund themselves. Workers resisted the new demands, and it was not until 1986 that a new working contract based on performance was introduced, and even this only applied to new workers. This meant that progress was sometimes slow, and production remained inefficient in the SOEs.

THE EMERGENCE OF PRIVATISATION AND WESTERNISATION

The changes in economic policy meant that China increasingly began to adopt Western ideas and behaviours. The SEZs were based on a system that Chinese officials had witnessed in travels to Taiwan, South Korea and even the Republic of Ireland. The SEZs relied on foreign technology and on Western business practices. Unlike the SOEs, the firms in the SEZs were really private businesses that were run to make profits. This type of privatisation also spread inland to businesses producing for the domestic market. Small-scale businesses were established in the countryside with few restrictions placed on production and distribution, which meant that they could sell goods for a profit outside their areas. They were known as Town and Village Enterprises (TVEs). By 1990, TVEs employed 100 million people.

Western influences were brought back to China via returning students and businessmen. Complaints were voiced that the younger generations were getting Western hairstyles and wearing Western clothes. Furthermore, they listened to 'decadent' Western music and seemed obsessed with making money. Some party members thought that the closer ties with the West were weakening the fundamental ideas of communism.

EXAM-STYLE QUESTION

A01   **A02**

Explain **two** ways in which Western influence in China in the years 1979–89 was similar to Western influence in China during the Qing dynasty in the years 1900–11.   **(6 marks)**

HINT

This question is about comparison. First of all, you will need to remind yourself about the role of Western powers in China in the years 1900–11 by reviewing the information in Chapter 1. When you have done that, you need to identify two similarities. Write a short paragraph for each of the factors that you have selected, explaining how they are similar.

BIRTH CONTROL

By 1979, China's population had grown to nearly 974 million. There were fears that its rapid expansion would make it impossible for economic policies to provide resources for the whole population. Therefore, the CCP introduced the 'one-child' policy. This was intended to limit the expansion of the population and ultimately reduce it in size. A new Marriage Law was passed, including the following.

■ The minimum age for marriage was set at 22 years for men and 20 years for women.
■ Married couples were allowed only one child.
■ There were financial penalties for going over this limit.

A couple had to get a permit to give birth. The state could order late-term abortions and sterilisations for women who already had one child. At first the policy was applied in the towns; a second child was allowed to peasants as long as there was a gap of 5 years between the first and second child.

▼ Andrew Ridgeley and George Michael from the British pop group Wham! meeting one of their Chinese fans during their visit to China in 1985

▶ A birth control poster advertising the one-child policy

There were significant problems with the policy, not least the increase in female infanticide. Peasant families continued to value a male child more than female because girls were less able to do heavy work in the fields and they married outside of the family, whereas a male child would have a responsibility to look after his parents in their old age.

The consequence of female infanticide, and the legal abortion of female foetuses, was a gender imbalance in the younger population. By 1985, there were 114 boys born to every 100 girls. The one-child policy was enforced by propaganda campaigns, 'struggle sessions' against parents of more than one child and the compulsory fitting of **contraceptive devices**. Couples who limited themselves to one child were rewarded. They received cash bonuses and extra rations. They were also given better treatment in health care and the education system, whereas those who did not follow the policy lost such privileges. The policy slowed down the growth of China's population.

SOURCE C

From the British newspaper, *The Observer*, commenting on the killing of Chinese baby girls in December 1982.

Chinese peasants are allowing their baby girls to die at such a rate that a call has gone out to save them. In some communes just 200 girls survive out of every 500 children born. The rise in killing of girls is a direct result of China's one-child family drive. Many Chinese still believe that without a son there can be no descendants. Only male children hand down the family name and can worship and nourish their ancestors.

EXTEND YOUR KNOWLEDGE

The one-child policy led to concerns about spoiled young boys growing up as 'little emperors' who received many gifts from parents and two sets of grandparents. But there were disadvantages too. As the boys grew up, they had to deal with excessive expectations. They were expected to excel academically and achieve high positions when they entered employment. Some of them experienced mental health issues as a result of the pressure. By the end of the 1990s, gangs emerged who stole young boys and sold them to rich couples who were desperate for a boy.

ACTIVITY

1 Study Source C. Make a list of the reasons that it suggests can explain the killing of baby girls.
2 Using the source and your knowledge, what were the consequences of the one-child policy for China?

5.3 DENG AND POLITICAL REFORM

LEARNING OBJECTIVES

■ Understand the reasons why Deng opposed political reform

■ Understand the Democracy Wall Movement and the role of Wei Jingsheng

■ Understand the origins of the Democracy Movement.

DENG'S OPPOSITION TO POLITICAL REFORM

KEY TERM

hard-line someone with a severe and tough attitude

Deng was prepared to be forward-thinking and introduce changes where the economy was concerned and to adopt capitalist practices if they succeeded in modernising the economy. However, in politics he remained a **hard-line** Communist, who would not move away from Marxist–Leninist ideas and Mao Zedong Thought. He maintained four principles about the way China would be governed.

■ The CCP would keep a leading role.

■ He rejected a multi-party system.

■ There would be no free elections.

■ There would be no freedom of speech.

In following these principles, he firmly rejected democracy (although he was also determined to remove corruption from the CCP). He was supported in his opposition to change by the older, more conservative members of the CCP.

THE 'DEMOCRACY WALL' MOVEMENT AND WEI JINGSHENG

There was a long brick wall in the Avenue of Eternal Peace near Tiananmen Square where people pinned letters and big character posters with their comments on what was happening in China. This wall became known as the Democracy Wall. At first, Deng was a supporter of the Democracy Wall. His supporters had pinned notes that supported Deng and criticised his opponents during the struggle to take power.

However, Deng's desire to maintain strict Communism was challenged when the wall was used by the people to express anti-government feelings. Students in particular used it to criticise the party and the lack of democracy. They were disappointed because they had thought that Deng would introduce democracy as a fifth modernisation when he became China's leader. In 1979, Wei Jingsheng, a former Red Guard, pinned to the wall his criticisms of the government's failure to allow democratic freedoms and accused the party of acting like the Qing dynasty. He was arrested and sentenced to 15 years in prison.

ACTIVITY

1 Study Source D. What criticisms does Wei Jingsheng make of the Communist Party?

2 Explain why Deng Xiaoping would see the Democracy Wall as a threat.

SOURCE D

From Wei Jingsheng's criticisms of the leadership of the CCP pinned on the Democracy Wall in 1979.

Those who worry that democracy will lead to anarchy and chaos are just like those who worried that without an emperor the country would fall into chaos... We need no gods or emperors... We do not want to serve as mere tools of dictators.

The Democracy Wall in Beijing in 1979, with big character posters.

THE ORIGINS OF THE DEMOCRACY MOVEMENT, 1979

Wei Jingsheng was one of those individuals whose brave stand inspired other activists to call for democracy in China. From 1979, intellectuals and students became involved in a Democracy Movement, which called for political reforms to match the modernisation in the economy. Many had experienced Western ideas of liberal politics when they had travelled abroad to study, and they wanted not just to end corruption in the CCP, but for the party to honour its claims that it represented the will of the people. It was from this Democracy Movement that more widespread demonstrations by Chinese students emerged in the mid-1980s and threatened to challenge the very existence of the Chinese Communist Party.

5.4 STUDENT OPPOSITION AND TIANANMEN SQUARE 1986–89

LEARNING OBJECTIVES

- Understand the aims and features of the students' protests
- Understand the reaction of Deng and the CCP
- Understand the reasons for and the results of the protest in Tiananmen Square in 1989.

In 1985, student demonstrations broke out in Beijing. These demonstrations spread, and by 1986 they were happening in universities across China.

THE AIMS AND FEATURES OF THE STUDENTS' PROTESTS

In Beijing, the initial protest was caused by the poor conditions in which the students lived and the high rents and prices that had been caused by the government's economic reforms. These problems were reflected in wider unrest and discontent expressed by workers by strikes. However, in the universities, criticisms of economic conditions were accompanied by political challenges to the government. The students blamed poor job prospects on the

ACTIVITY

Imagine you are a student protestor. Create a big character poster for the Democracy Wall. Make sure you cover all of your criticisms of Deng's government.

party, saying that it gave better treatment in employment to family members and friends instead of hiring on merit. Students were also angry about the way the government placed controls on what they were allowed to study and which books they could read.

The students came to believe that there was something essentially corrupt about the CCP and, using big character posters, they called for the introduction of democracy in China and for free speech. Some called for a multi-party system and free elections. In other words, they wanted an end to the 'dictatorship' of the Chinese Communist Party.

THE REACTION OF DENG AND THE CCP

The traditionalist members in the CCP were angered by the students' criticisms. When the general secretary of the party, Hu Yaobang, seemed to show sympathy for the students by criticising the slow pace of reform, he was sacked. In sacking him, Deng showed that he sided with the hard-line conservatives who would not accept any move away from Maoist Communism.

Censorship was tightened further, and Deng ordered the arrest of the leaders whom he blamed for the unrest. He announced that China did not need democracy, because the people had an enlightened government to rule for them. While this **repression** and tough approach ended the 1986 protests, it did not address the concerns of the peasants and workers. It only created resentment, which led to protests once again in 1989.

TIANANMEN SQUARE, 1989

The protests in 1989 were started by the death of Hu Yaobang from a heart attack in April. Students, remembering how he had been sacked for appearing to support the 1986 protests, gathered in large numbers in Tiananmen Square to express sadness about Hu Yaobang's death. The numbers grew further still when the Premier Li Peng refused to accept a petition asking for greater freedoms. The seriousness of the demonstration was shown by the fact that transport workers allowed students to travel to Beijing for free on public transport. This was a clear sign that the students had support among other groups in the country. The students organised sit-ins and by May 1989, 300 of them had begun a hunger strike. There were frequent fights with the police and calls from the national newspaper, the *People's Daily*, for the government to end the protest.

SOURCE F

From the students' statement about their hunger strike which was handed out before they began the strike on 13 May 1989.

We ask all citizens of China, every worker, peasant, soldier, average person, intellectual, government official, policeman and all of those who have made up charges against us: Put your hands over your own hearts and ask your own consciences, what crime have we committed? Are we creating 'turmoil'? We are boycotting classes, we are demonstrating, we are engaging [taking part] in a hunger strike … Why are we doing all of this? … Student representatives knelt down to beg for democracy but were ignored.

The reaction of the Communist Party to the protest was complicated by the planned visit of President Gorbachev from the Soviet Union. The eyes of the world were fixed on China as thousands of journalists hurried into the capital to report on the event. It was not the best time for Deng to deal severely with the protestors. Therefore, instead of taking action to deal with the protestors, Deng reorganised the schedule for Gorbachev's meeting to make sure he didn't see what was happening in Tiananmen Square.

SOURCE G

A young man standing in front of a convoy of tanks in the Avenue of Eternal Peace, Tiananmen Square, during the student protests in June 1989. This iconic image was beamed across the world as a symbol of the bravery of the young man who is known only as 'tankman'. It is not known what happened to him when the protest was ended.

EXTEND YOUR KNOWLEDGE

President Mikhail Gorbachev had introduced reforms into the Soviet Union that gave greater freedom of expression. By removing from the Soviet Constitution the absolute right of the Communist Party to rule, he had put the Soviet Union on the path to democracy. These were the type of changes that protestors in China wanted the CCP to introduce.

President Mikhail Gorbachev and his wife with Deng Xiaoping on his visit to China in 1989.

martial law the temporary end to ordinary law and the enforcement of control by the military. All power is removed from other branches of the government

Gorbachev returned to the Soviet Union on 19 May. Deng then declared **martial law** in China. However, the situation became even more serious when the non-student population of Beijing began to join the student protest. They shouted, 'We want democracy! We want Deng to go!' These protestors blocked the roads and prevented the troops stationed around Beijing from getting to Tiananmen Square. This delayed the attempts of the government to 'restore order', but could not prevent the government from ending the protest. By 2 June, 350,000 PLA troops surrounded Tiananmen Square, and on 3 June, the government announced that the Square would be cleared by the following morning.

The protestors resisted attempts to clear them from the Square. In a night of violence, soldiers in tanks and armoured vehicles opened fire on them. The numbers killed will never be known, but it was certainly in the thousands. In the weeks afterwards, suspects were arrested and sentenced to prison. Any member of the Chinese Communist Party who had shown sympathy for the peasants was dismissed from office.

The events in Tiananmen Square demonstrated Deng's determination to destroy the opposition and end once and for all the calls for political reform. In taking this action against the students, Deng had acted just as previous rulers had done when they faced with opposition. He had been prepared to reform Mao's economic policy, but as far as the government was concerned, China in 1989 was to be governed according to Mao's beliefs. Whatever the protestors in Tiananmen Square might have hoped for, this rule did not include democracy and political freedom.

SOURCE I

From Deng Xiaoping's speech to the officers who enforced the martial law in Beijing, 9 June 1989.

The main difficulty in handling this matter is that we never experienced such a situation before, in which a small minority of bad people mixed with so many young students and onlookers. We did not have a clear picture of the situation, and this prevented us from taking some actions that we should have taken earlier...

The nature of the matter became clear soon after it erupted. They had two main slogans: to overthrow the Communist Party and topple the socialist system. Their goal was to establish a bourgeois republic entirely dependent on the West. Of course we accept people's demands for combating corruption. We are even ready to listen to some persons with ulterior motives when they raise the slogan about fighting corruption. However, such slogans were just a front. Their real aim was to overthrow the Communist Party and topple the socialist system.

EXTRACT A

From an assessment of Deng's actions in Tiananmen Square, written in a history of China, published 2013.

Deng joined the Dowager Empress, Yuan Shikai, Ching Kai-shek and Mao Zedong as a man who clamped down on freedom if it appeared to threaten the form of regime he headed and thereby his own position.

EXAM-STYLE QUESTION

A01 **A02**

SKILLS ▶ ADAPTIVE LEARNING

Explain **two** causes of Deng's decision to use violence to end the protest in Tiananmen Square in 1989. **(8 marks)**

HINT

This question is about causation. When explaining the reasons why something happened, you should identify two reasons and write a paragraph for each reason, giving some precise details to explain how it led to the outcome.

THE RESULTS OF TIANANMEN SQUARE

The international reaction to the events in Tiananmen Square was one of universal condemnation and disapproval. The Soviet Union announced that it was greatly saddened by the events and wished that 'China's leaders had chosen to handle the situation differently', while the USA introduced **economic sanctions** against China. It was 10 years before another American president visited China.

The events in Tiananmen Square remain a difficult issue to this day. The Chinese governments that followed have refused to explain the massacre or hold any of the offenders responsible for it. Shortly after the event, Deng's government claimed that it was a **legitimate** attack on 'counter-revolutionaries', and since then, the event has been described by Chinese governments as merely 'political turmoil' and not needing further investigation. Although economic reforms have continued, the government continues to strictly limit the freedoms of speech and expression. In the 21st century, this has included a strict control over the internet.

ACTIVITY

1 'The student was really foolish to stand in front of the tank.' Do you agree? Explain your answer.
2 Study Source I. How did Deng justify the action taken by the army against the protestors?
3 Why do you think we don't know how many died?

RECAP

RECALL QUESTIONS

1 List two reasons why the Gang of Four believed it would take power after Mao's death.
2 Why did Deng Xiaoping emerge as the leader of China in 1978?
3 Why was the increase in agricultural output lower than Deng had expected?
4 What was an SEZ?
5 In what ways was Deng's economic policy similar to capitalism?
6 Give one reason why the one-child policy led to female infanticide.
7 What was the Democracy Wall?
8 Give three reasons why students opposed Deng's government.
9 Why did Deng delay ending the protest in Tiananmen Square?
10 List two consequences of the protest in Tiananmen Square.

CHECKPOINT

STRENGTHEN

S1 Write a paragraph explaining the fall of the Gang of Four.
S2 In what ways did Western ideas have a greater influence in China in the years 1978–89?
S3 List three ways in which students opposed the communist system under Deng.

CHALLENGE

C1 What were the consequences of the CCP's economic policies on agricultural and industrial production?
C2 Compare the impact of Mao's and Deng's Marriage Laws on the lives of women. Draw a spider diagram using two colours: one for positive impacts and the other for negative impacts. Which law was more beneficial for women? Suggest two reasons to explain the difference.
C3 How far had China changed from a communist system to a capitalist system under Deng? Draw up a table with two columns: one headed 'Communist' and the other 'Capitalist'. List the communist and capitalist features in each column. Use the table to help you write a judgement addressing the question of 'how far'.

SUMMARY

- The Gang of Four expected to rule after Mao's death, but lacked support in both the CCP and the PLA.
- Deng Xiaoping was named as the leader of China in October 1978.
- Deng aimed to modernise the Chinese economy by allowing more private ownership and profit incentives, and by adopting Western technology and production methods.
- The xiang replaced the collective, and peasants were allowed to lease land and sell extra produce for a profit after meeting targets. This led to increases in production.
- Higher education was expanded and young people were encouraged to study abroad, where they would learn about Western technology.
- Industry was modernised by the establishment of SEZs that focused on producing goods for export, by expanding trade links with the West and by reducing government support for SOEs.
- A one-child policy was introduced to control the rate at which China's population was growing, but this led to increased incidents of female infanticide.
- Deng was a hard-line conservative in politics, and he resisted calls for democracy in the Democracy Movement in the 1980s.
- Deng authorised the massacre of students and workers demonstrating for democracy in Tiananmen Square in June 1989.

EXAM GUIDANCE: PART (C) QUESTIONS

A01   **A02**

SKILLS ▶ PROBLEM SOLVING, REASONING, DECISION MAKING

Question to be answered: How far did the organisation of agriculture in China change in the years 1949–89?

You may use the following in your answer:
- the Agrarian Reform Law 1950
- changes under Deng Xiaoping.

You **must** also use information of your own.   **(16 marks)**

1 **Analysis Question 1: What is the question type testing?**
In this question, you have to demonstrate that you have knowledge and understanding of the key features and characteristics of the period studied. In this particular case, it is knowledge and understanding of the organisation of agriculture in the years 1949–89.

You also have to explain, analyse and make judgements about historical events and periods to give an explanation and reach a judgement on the role of various factors in bringing about changes.

2 **Analysis Question 2: What do I have to do to answer the question well?**
- You have been given two factors on which to write. You don't have to use them and can provide your own factors. (But it seems sensible to do so!)
- However, you must avoid just giving the information. What changes did these events cause?
- You are also asked 'how far' the organisation of agriculture changed. So when discussing these events, you need to consider whether the organisation changed or whether the evidence suggests it mainly stayed the same.
- You will also see that the question says you must use information of your own. So that should include at least one factor other than those you have been given.
- That factor might be Mutual Aid Teams or Mao's collectivisation programme, for example.

3 **Analysis Question 3: Are there any techniques I can use to make it very clear that I am doing what is needed to be successful?**
This is a 16-mark question and you need to make sure you give a substantial answer. You will be up against time pressures, so here are some useful techniques to help you succeed.
- Do not write a lengthy introduction. Give a brief introduction which answers the question straight away and shows what your paragraphs are going to be about.
- To make sure you stay focused on the question and avoid just writing narrative, try to use the words of the question at the beginning of each paragraph.
- Remember that this question is a change question, so make sure what you are writing about explains why this did or did not mean change.

Answer

Here is a student response to the question. The teacher has made some comments.

Where is your introduction? What is missing is a short overview of the whole answer. This could be achieved by looking at the opening sentences of each of the paragraphs below: together they should add up to an overview.

There were some very importance changes in the organisation of agriculture in China in the years 1949–89. Mao wanted to bring about big changes for peasants who had been badly treated by landlords before the Communists took power. In 1950 his government introduced the Agrarian Reform Law. This law took away the land that was held by large landlords and gave it to the peasants. This was a great change for the peasants because it meant that they now had their own land and the rich landlords who had bullied the peasants were destroyed. Thousands of rich land lords were sent to special camps to be re-educated about communism. However, the change in the organisation was not very great because the land was still owned by private individuals. It was just that it had swapped hands from rich landlords to the peasants.

This is a great paragraph. It has an opening sentence which explains what the paragraph is about – the point of the paragraph – and it then uses detailed knowledge to support the point. And you have considered 'how far' by showing what had stayed the same! Well done.

There were even more important changes introduced after 1950. First of all peasants were encouraged to join mutual aid teams and pool their land, animals and equipment and farm the land together. These mutual aid teams were usually made up of about ten households. This was a stage towards a communist organisation of agriculture in which there was no private ownership and all the land was held owned by the state, but at that time the peasants still owned the land. Further changes were introduced with the APCs where mutual aid teams grouped together and could use large machinery on the land because of their large size. Finally, in the years 1956–58, Mao began to introduce the system of collectivisation in agriculture. Huge collective farms of 2,000–3,000 households were set up. All the land, the animals and the equipment belonged to the collective farm and private ownership was ended. So from 1949 to 1958 a really big change had occurred in agriculture.

Another good paragraph. You answer the question, give contextual knowledge and develop both changes and continuities so you are really addressing the 'how far' part of the question. However, a touch more is sometimes needed. For example: How many mutual aid teams grouped together in the APCs? When did the APCs begin to develop?

In conclusion, there were very important changes to the system of agriculture in the years 1949–89. Under Mao, the system changed from one of private ownership to a communist system where all the land was owned by the state and the peasants belonged to a collective. Peasants did not like the collective system, so under Deng the system was changed again to give them more freedom to work hard and make a profit. It is interesting that there was a major change, but in the end some things stayed nearly the same because the peasants had been able to make profits before Mao came to power.

Good – a focused finish which shows change over time and makes it clear that there were also some things that remained similar to the system that existed when Mao came to power in 1949.

What are the strengths and weaknesses of this answer?
You can see the strengths and weaknesses of this answer from what the teacher says. If there had been three paragraphs like the one on the Agrarian Reform Law, this would have been an excellent answer.

Work with a friend
Discuss with a friend how you would turn the weaker paragraphs into ones that would enable the whole answer to get very high marks.

Use the Student Book to set another part (c) question on this period for a friend. Then look at the answer. Does it do the following things?

☐ Identify changes across at least a large part of the period 1949–89
☐ Provide detailed information to explain where there was change or no change
☐ Provide at least one factor other than those given in the question
☐ Address 'how far?'

A NOTE ON THE USE OF CHINESE SPELLING

At the beginning of the 20th century, Western countries used the Giles-Wade system of spelling Chinese names and places. The Giles-Wade system is a phonetic system that spells words the way that they sound. In the late 1950s, the Hanyu Pinyin system was used to convert Mandarin Chinese into Western (or Roman, as it is officially known) spellings. Most Western student books now use the Pinyin system, but it is not used by every historian. In some cases, books use a mixture of Giles-Wade and Pinyin, especially where a name is so well known that it would be confusing for Western readers to see it in Pinyin. The table below shows the variations in the spelling of the most common words used in this book.

▼ PINYIN	▼ GILES-WADE
Beijing	Peking
Chen Boda	Ch'en Po-ta
Guomindang (GMD)	Kuomintang (KMT)
Hua Guofeng	Hua Kuo-feng
Jiang Jieshi	Chiang Kai-shek
Jiang Qing	Jiang Ch'ing
Jiangsi	Kiangsi
Lin Biao	Lin Piao
Liu Shaoqi	Liu Shao-ch'i
Mao Zedong	Mao Tse tung
Nanjing	Nanking
Sun Zhong Shan	Sun Yat-sen
Wei Jingsheng	Wei Ching-sheng
Zhou Enlai	Chou Enlai

GLOSSARY

abdicate to give up the position of being king or queen

abortion a medical operation to end a pregnancy

atomic bomb a bomb with enormous destructive power, due to the sudden release of energy caused by the splitting of the nuclei of the chemical plutonium or uranium

baptise to accept someone as a member of a particular Christian church by a ceremony of baptism

besiege to surround a city or castle with military force until the people inside let you take control

black market the illegal trade of goods

blockade the surrounding of an area by soldiers or ships to stop people or supplies entering or leaving

bourgeoisie the people in a society who are rich, educated, own land, etc., according to Marxism

Buddhism a religion of east and central Asia, based on the teaching of Gautama Buddha

bureaucrat someone who works in a bureaucracy and uses official rules very strictly

cadre a group of activists

capitalism an economic and political system in which businesses belong mostly to private owners, not to the government

censorship the practice or system of censoring something (examining books, films, letters, etc. to remove anything that is considered offensive, morally harmful or politically dangerous).

chain of command a system in army or government organisations by which instructions are passed from one person to another

Christianity the religion based on the life and beliefs of Jesus Christ

collective a group of people who work together to run something such as a business or farm, and who share the profits equally

communist someone who is a member of a political party that supports communism, or who believes in communism – a political system in which the government controls the production of all food and goods, and there is no privately owned property

compensation money paid to someone because they have suffered injury or loss, or because something they own has been damaged

comradeship the development of company and friendship with others who share similar views

concession something that you allow someone to have in order to end an argument or a disagreement

concubine the practice of keeping women as mistresses. The concubine would be in a sexual relationship with the man and often live alongside the wife but be ranked as having lower status

Confucianism a Chinese way of thought which teaches that you should be loyal to your family, friends, and rulers and treat others as you would like to be treated. Confucianism was developed from the ideas of Confucius

conscript the compulsory enlistment of men into the armed forces

conservative not liking changes or new ideas

constitution a set of basic laws and principles by which a country or organisation is governed

contraceptive device a method to prevent pregnancy

cult of personality a situation in which people are encouraged to admire and praise a famous person, especially a political leader

dam a special wall built across a river or stream to stop the water from flowing, especially in order to make a lake or produce electricity

dictator a ruler who has complete power over a country, especially one whose power has been gained by force

distribution the act of sharing things among a large group of people in a planned way

dowager the widow of an emperor, king or duke

dowry the money and other goods that were given to by the bride's family to the husband's family to settle the marriage. It was sometimes called the 'bride-price'

dynasty a family of kings or other rulers whose parents, grandparents, etc. have ruled the country for many years

economic sanction measure taken to damage a country's economy, usually involving a trade ban

emperor the man who is the ruler of an empire

empire a group of countries that are all controlled by one ruler or government

empress a female ruler of an empire, or the wife of an emperor

enlightenment when you understand something clearly, or when you help someone do this

fraud the crime of deceiving people in order to gain something such as money or goods

free speech the right to express any opinions without fear of punishment

general strike a situation when most of the workers in a country refuse to work in order to protest about working conditions, wages, etc.

H-bomb a nuclear weapon that takes its energy from the fusion of hydrogen elements

inflation rising prices and a fall in the value of money

intellectual an intellectual person is well-educated and interested in serious ideas and subjects such as science, literature, etc.

left-wing a left-wing person or group supports the political aims of groups, such as socialists and communists

legitimate acceptable or allowed by law

Mandate of Heaven a belief used to justify the rule of the emperor

martyr a person who is killed because of their beliefs

middle class the social class that includes people who are educated and work in professional jobs, for example, teachers or managers

missionaries people who have been sent to a foreign country to teach others about Christianity and persuade them to become Christians

mutiny a rebellion by soldiers or sailors against their commanding officers

mutual aid team team of people sharing resources such as tools, labour and capital on a temporary or permanent basis

nationalist a nationalist organisation, party or person wants to gain or keep political independence for their country and people

opium a powerful illegal drug made from poppy seeds. Drugs made from opium are used to reduce severe pain

overthrow (overthrown) to remove a leader or government from power, especially by force

peasants poor farmers who own or rent a small amount of land, either in past times or in poor countries

petroleum oil that is obtained from below the surface of the Earth and is used to make petrol, paraffin and various chemical substances

private (enterprise) the economic system in which private businesses are allowed to compete freely with each other, and the government does not control industry

privatisation the act of privatising something. If a government privatises an organisation, industry, or service that it owns or controls, it sells it

propaganda the deliberate use of information and ideas to promote a particular point of view

province one of the large areas into which some countries are divided, and which usually has its own local government

puppet state a state that allows others to control it and to make its decisions

quota an official limit on the number or amount of something that is allowed in a particular period

radical radical ideas are very new and different, and are against what most people think or believe

rationing when the amount of food, petrol, etc. that people are allowed to have is limited by the government

regent someone who governs instead of a king or queen, because the king or queen is ill, absent or still a child

regime a government, especially one that was not elected fairly or that you disapprove of for some other reason

reparation when you give something to someone or do something for them because you have done something wrong to them in the past

repression cruel and severe control of a large group of people

republic a country governed by elected representatives of the people, and led by a president, not a king or queen

sabotage to secretly damage or destroy equipment, vehicles, etc. that belong to an enemy or opponent, so that they cannot be used

static war a war where both sides suffer heavy losses and the advance or retreat is so slow that the war appears 'static' (showing a lack of change)

sterilisation if a person or animal is sterilised, they have an operation to stop them producing babies

succession the act of taking over an official job or position, or the right to be the next to take it

superpower a nation that has very great military and political power

supply lines the different ways, places, etc. that an army uses to send food and equipment to its soldiers during a war

treaty a formal written agreement between two or more countries or governments

warlord the leader of an unofficial military group fighting against a government, king or different group

working class the group of people in society who traditionally do physical work and do not have much money or power

INDEX